Jump Start Responsive Web Design, 2nd Ed

by Chris Ward

Copyright © 2017 SitePoint Pty. Ltd.

Product Manager: Simon Mackie **Technical Editor:** Craig Buckler
English Editor: Ralph Mason **Cover Designer:** Alex Walker

Notice of Rights

All rights reserved. No part of this book may be reproduced, stored in a retrieval system or transmitted in any form or by any means, without the prior written permission of the publisher, except in the case of brief quotations embodied in critical articles or reviews.

Notice of Liability

The author and publisher have made every effort to ensure the accuracy of the information herein. However, the information contained in this book is sold without warranty, either express or implied. Neither the authors and SitePoint Pty. Ltd., nor its dealers or distributors will be held liable for any damages to be caused either directly or indirectly by the instructions contained in this book, or by the software or hardware products described herein.

Trademark Notice

Rather than indicating every occurrence of a trademarked name as such, this book uses the names only in an editorial fashion and to the benefit of the trademark owner with no intention of infringement of the trademark.

Published by SitePoint Pty. Ltd.

48 Cambridge Street Collingwood
VIC Australia 3066
Web: www.sitepoint.com
Email: books@sitepoint.com

ISBN 978-0-9943470-9-1 (print)

ISBN 978-0-9953827-2-5 (ebook)
Printed and bound in the United States of America

About Chris Ward

Chris explains cool tech to the World. He's a technical writer and blogger. He has crazy projects in progress and will speak to anyone who listens.

About SitePoint

SitePoint specializes in publishing fun, practical, and easy-to-understand content for web professionals. Visit http://www.sitepoint.com/ to access our blogs, books, newsletters, articles, and community forums. You'll find a stack of information on JavaScript, PHP, Ruby, mobile development, design, and more.

This book is dedicated to 2016, as that was the year I was supposed to finish it, but life got in the way. It was also a pretty interesting year, wasn't it?

I should probably also dedicate this book to my wife for putting up constantly with "Can't do anything this weekend, got to work on the book."

Table of Contents

Preface ix
Who Should Read This Book ix
Conventions Used ix
    Tips, Notes, and Warnings xi
Supplementary Materials xi

Chapter 1 The Meaning and Purpose of Responsive Web Design 1
History 5
Schools of Thought Within Responsive Design 6
    Progressive Enhancement 6
    Graceful Degradation 6
    Mobile First 6
What Do You Need To Support? 7
    Computers 7
    Mobile Phones 8
    Tablets 8
    Hybrid Devices 8

Wearables 9

TV 9

Cars 9

Game Consoles 9

Print 10

Sample Application 10

Introducing RWDFlix 10

Computer Version 10

Tablet Version 11

Mobile Version 12

TV Version 13

Structuring a Page with HTML5 14

Ready to Respond? 20

Chapter 2   The Building Blocks of Responsive Design 21

Media Types 22

Creating a Query 23

Logical Queries with Only and Not 28

Query Features 29

Streamlining the Example App 32

Mobile First 38

The Viewport Meta Element 39

Any Queries? 46

Chapter 3   Better Responsive Structures with Grid Systems 47

What Is a Grid? 53

Creating Your Own Grid 54

Flexbox 65

CSS Grid Layout 71

Making Grids Easier with Frameworks 79

    Bootstrap 79

    Foundation 81

What About the Demo App? 82

Wrap Up 83

Chapter 4   Responsive Text 84

The History of Text 84

Responsive Typographical Properties in CSS 86

    Fixed Sizing 88

Relative Sizing 91

Creating Readable Text 99

Read On 103

Chapter 5 Responsive Images and Video 104

Images 105

Responsive Dimensions 109

The Right Image for the Right Device 111

`srcset` 112

The `picture` Element 114

Responsive Video 116

The `video` Element 116

Get Visual 126

Chapter 6 Responding to User Context 127

An API for Everything 127

Based on Time 128

Battery Level 130

Geolocation 135

Based on Network 138

User Preference 139

Ambient Light 140

Vibration 144

Device Orientation 145

Responding to All 151

Preface

The pixel-perfect web is dead. The days of positioning elements on a web page and expecting them to always display how we wanted are a distant memory; we now cope with the constant barrage of new and varied devices that our designs need to look fantastic on.

This book aims to get you started understanding and using the suite of CSS and HTML tools for responding to this new world of devices. It will introduce you to the building blocks that help your pages adapt to different devices, take this a step further with grids, show you how to make text and images readable on all devices, and, in the final chapter, cover how to utilize more esoteric device capabilities.

Let's get started.

Who Should Read This Book

This book is for web designers and front-end developers. You'll need to be familiar with HTML and CSS, but no previous responsive web design experience is required. Some JavaScript familiarity is useful for the latter parts of the book.

Conventions Used

You'll notice that we've used certain typographic and layout styles throughout this book to signify different types of information. Look out for the following items.

Code Samples

Code in this book is displayed using a fixed-width font, like so:

```
<h1>A Perfect Summer's Day</h1>
  <p>It was a lovely day for a walk in the park. The
```

```
↳ birds were singing and the kids were all back at
↳ school.</p>
```

If the code is to be found in the book's code archive, the name of the file will appear at the top of the program listing, like this:

0-1. example.css

```
.footer {
  background-color: #CCC;
  border-top: 1px solid #333;
}
```

If only part of the file is displayed, this is indicated by the word *excerpt*:

0-2. example.css (excerpt)

```
.footer {
  background-color: #CCC;
  border-top: 1px solid #333;
}
```

If additional code is to be inserted into an existing example, the new code will be displayed in bold:

```
function animate() {
  new_variable = "Hello";
}
```

Where existing code is required for context, rather than repeat all of it, ⋮ will be displayed:

```
function animate() {
  ⋮
  new_variable = "Hello";
```

```
}
```

Some lines of code should be entered on one line, but we've had to wrap them because of page constraints. An ↪ indicates a line break that exists for formatting purposes only, and should be ignored:

```
URL.open("http://www.sitepoint.com/responsive-web-design-real
↪ -user-testing/?responsive1");
```

Tips, Notes, and Warnings

 Hey, You!

Tips provide helpful little pointers.

 Ahem, Excuse Me ...

Notes are useful asides that are related—but not critical—to the topic at hand. Think of them as extra tidbits of information.

 Make Sure You Always ...

... pay attention to these important points.

 Watch Out!

Warnings highlight any gotchas that are likely to trip you up along the way.

Supplementary Materials

- The book's code archive contains downloadable code and sample videos to accompany the examples presented.
- https://www.sitepoint.com/community/ are SitePoint's forums, for help on any tricky web problems.

■ **books@sitepoint.com** is our email address, should you need to contact us to report a problem, or for any other reason.

Chapter 1

The Meaning and Purpose of Responsive Web Design

It used to be so simple: you'd design a website or application for a 15-inch monitor, and—incompatibilities between browsers aside—you were done.

Then mobile phones with web browsers came along and ruined our easy lives. Worst of all, people loved browsing the Web on them!

 The Rise of Mobile

In 2016, browsing the web on mobile devices overtook desktop browsing[1] for the first time.

---

[1] https://www.sitepoint.com/browser-trends-december-2016-mobile-overtakes-desktop/

Just as developers and designers got used to building websites for phones, along came tablets, watches, TVs, cars, glasses, larger desktop screens, high-resolution screens, and even web browsers built into walls. (Okay, I made that last one up.) Supporting this seemingly endless stream of new devices is becoming ever more challenging.

So how do we support this ever-increasing array of devices? The answer is *responsive web design*, which harnesses technologies that allow websites to adapt to screens of all sizes.

A lot of older sites, or projects maintained by people with little spare time, are unresponsive. For example, the site for the Vassal game engine:

The Meaning and Purpose of Responsive Web Design 3

1-3. The Vassal website is unresponsive

Many other sites, like SitePoint.com, are fully responsive:

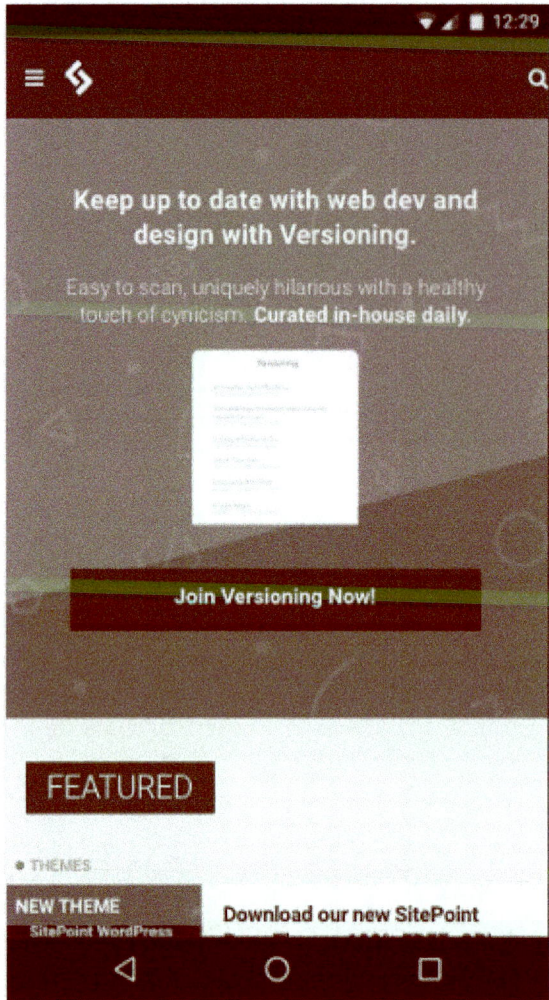

1-4. SitePoint.com is responsive, valuing readers on all devices

Responsive web design (RWD) subscribes to the popular development maxim "Don't Repeat Yourself" (usually abbreviated to "DRY"). Instead of maintaining multiple codebases for each device that you wish to support, RWD aims to use a single codebase that adapts appropriately to each device. Using RWD techniques, you write one set of HTML, CSS, and JavaScript, and display elements appropriately for each platform. Many of these styles and elements can even be reused or built upon for maximum code efficiency.

Sound good to you? To begin, let's go back in time a few years.

History

"Responsive" design is not necessarily new and is a term that can mean different things to different people, making its exact history hard to track down.

In theory, developers have been creating responsive designs since there was more than one browser. Browsers have always had subtle (and not so subtle) rendering differences between them, and developers have been learning how to cope with these quirks for decades. If you're new(er) to web development, be thankful the dominance of Internet Explorer's earlier versions is mostly over. The days of dealing with their quirks were dark.

Since 2004, responsive design has adopted the more specific meaning of adapting your designs to suit a user's device of choice—typically based on screen size, but also other capabilities. The concepts for responsive design solidified in 2008, but the term is also referred to as "flexible", "liquid", "fluid", and "elastic" design.

It was the inclusion of media queries in the CSS3 specification that fully gave responsive design the potential it needed to be a genuine and more usable concept. We'll cover media queries in detail in Chapter 2, but in summary, they allow you to change what you show in a web page based on pre-defined screen sizes or types. Ethan Marcotte formally coined the term "responsive web design" in an article for A List Apart[2] in 2010.

This led to a growth and consolidation of other techniques and technologies alongside media queries, such as flexible images and grids, all of which we'll cover in this book.

To me, "responsive design" is something of a combination of all these ideas and principles. It's not just adapting a design to screen sizes, but also to other factors such as color depth, media type (say, a laptop screen, or an eReader), or location.

[2.] http://alistapart.com/article/responsive-web-design

Schools of Thought Within Responsive Design

There are as many schools of thought about how to use responsive design as there are interpretations of it. Some have come and gone, and others have stuck. We won't cover any in detail explicitly in this book, but we'll touch upon their practical applications. Let's quickly cover a few of them now.

Progressive Enhancement

When following the more traditional principle of **progressive enhancement**, your primary focus is on making the site content available to all users, however simple their device or slow their connection. Then extra features—such as more sophisticated design and functionality—are added for devices that can utilize them.

Graceful Degradation

The proliferation of mobile browsing has reversed the more traditional path of design. In the past, you started a design on the platform you worked on (typically a computer) and then stripped away style and functionality to support devices with smaller screens or less support for certain features.

While **graceful degradation** is typically applied to the lack of browser support for particular features, you can also think of it more generally. Its principle is that you start with a fully featured version of a site, running on your ideal device and browser, while also ensuring that essential functionality will work for any user on any (supported) device, even if they lose out on nice-to-have features.

Mobile First

Mobile first is similar to progressive enhancement, but more specific to responsive design. It proposes that you start with your smallest or least capable supported device (typically a phone when the principle was created) and then add functionality and style as you increase the device scale.

 Mobile First

As a term, "mobile first" can be confusing, especially to non-designer/developer audiences, giving a skewed impression of the priority that mobile will receive in a project.

In theory, the practice ensures that smaller devices don't end up getting second best—that all devices are treated with equal importance.

What Do You Need To Support?

Before starting or enhancing any web-based project, it's important to know if it's worthwhile, and to assess the (potential) userbase for all your hard work.

If you have an existing website, it may be worth analyzing website traffic to see what types of devices your visitors are using to access your website. If 90% of visitors have consistently visited on a desktop machine, this shows that either your mobile experience is poor, or that your visitors are not big mobile device users. You could embark on extensive research to find out the exact answer, or simply use responsive design techniques to build a mobile-friendly site that may attract new visitors.

If you're working on a new project, analyzing the needs of your potential users is equally important. This can be done by using traditional market research techniques, creating simple test sites, or looking at your competitors to build a picture of who your customers will be.

Computers

Despite the slow decline in sales, there are still lots of desktop and laptop computers out there, and lots of web browsers running on them. These computers include everything from low-quality (and low-resolution) 11-inch netbooks to high-powered desktops with 28-inch, high-resolution monitors in a variety of proportions and orientations, all of which greatly affect the screen area you have to work with.

Mobile Phones

The percentage of people browsing websites on mobile phones has now reached parity with desktop browsing, so catering for users of mobile browsers is of equal (and likely, growing) importance.

 Mobile Browsing Stats

For more details on the rise of mobile web browsing, I recommend the Smart Insights report on Mobile Marketing Statistics[3] and Statcounter's desktop and mobile usage comparison[4].

On iOS, this is generally through just one browser, and the device's sizes are more consistent.

Android has a wide variety of browsers and screen dimensions available. Increasing numbers of devices running mobile operating systems also have high-density screens of varying resolutions.

You also need to consider that users are largely browsing with touch and not point-and-click devices, which affects behavior a great deal.

Tablets

Tablet sales may be shrinking, but there will still be a significant userbase for the foreseeable future, and you shouldn't think of tablets as large mobile phones or small desktops. Also, users may be using touch screens or mice to interact with your site.

Hybrid Devices

If handling computers and tablets wasn't enough for you, there are now hybrid devices, such as Microsoft's Surface Pro, that can switch between being a

---

[3] http://www.smartinsights.com/mobile-marketing/mobile-marketing-analytics/mobile-marketing-statistics/
[4] http://gs.statcounter.com/platform-market-share/desktop-mobile/worldwide/#monthly-201501-201706

computer and a tablet. While each mode can be treated discretely, it's worth noting that users may switch context while using your site.

Wearables

Most wearables are yet to gain a web browser, but it may happen. In the meantime, it's still possible to re-purpose parts of your content on wearables, and these will need to be delivered in short bursts with an easy follow-up action.

TV

Smart TVs and related devices such as Apple TV come with simplified web browsers, and users will generally use them for browsing particular sites, but they're likely to become increasingly popular. TVs have very large screens, often with low resolution, so sites viewed on them need to be clear enough to see properly and also usable from a distance.

Cars

Really? Yes, really. This is new territory, but an increasing number of cars now have dashboards with access to the internet in some form or another. For the time being, sites rendered on car dashboards will need to present information clearly on a small screen, and be designed not to distract or overwhelm a driver and thus cause an accident. However, many cars now have screens for passengers, who will have much fuller access to the web and content.

Game Consoles

Most modern game consoles spend some of their time connected to the internet, and some of that time with a web browser. This is typically for media consumption and social networks. Browsers on these devices will likely be limited, and a physical keyboard may not be available. For home consoles, design principles from TV will apply, and for handhelds, a limited mobile experience.

In summary, you can't predict how and where anyone will view your website, so build it to be adaptable, flexible, and responsive.

Print

Print? Isn't this a web design book? Yes, but print versions of your web pages will still be frequently accessed, whether for actual physical printing or for rendering your content on offline readers such as Instapaper or Pocket. For certain content, "print" is still relevant.

 Books, Too

> The page you're reading was also rendered with HTML and CSS. Yes, even the dead tree version.

Sample Application

In my experience, learning by example is always the best way to learn, so for this book, we'll create a demo website and optimize it for the wide range of devices it might be accessed on. In each chapter, we'll build upon the same website to illustrate the topic under discussion.

Introducing RWDFlix

RWDFlix is a fictional video streaming service that contains local, national and global TV shows for people to watch online. Which shows a user can watch will depend on their location and the time of day.

Computer Version

The layout of the site for desktop computers will show image thumbnails, a video player, a title of the program, the length of the video, and a description of the show. While network speeds vary less for desktop users, this version will check for sufficient bandwidth before letting the user play a video.

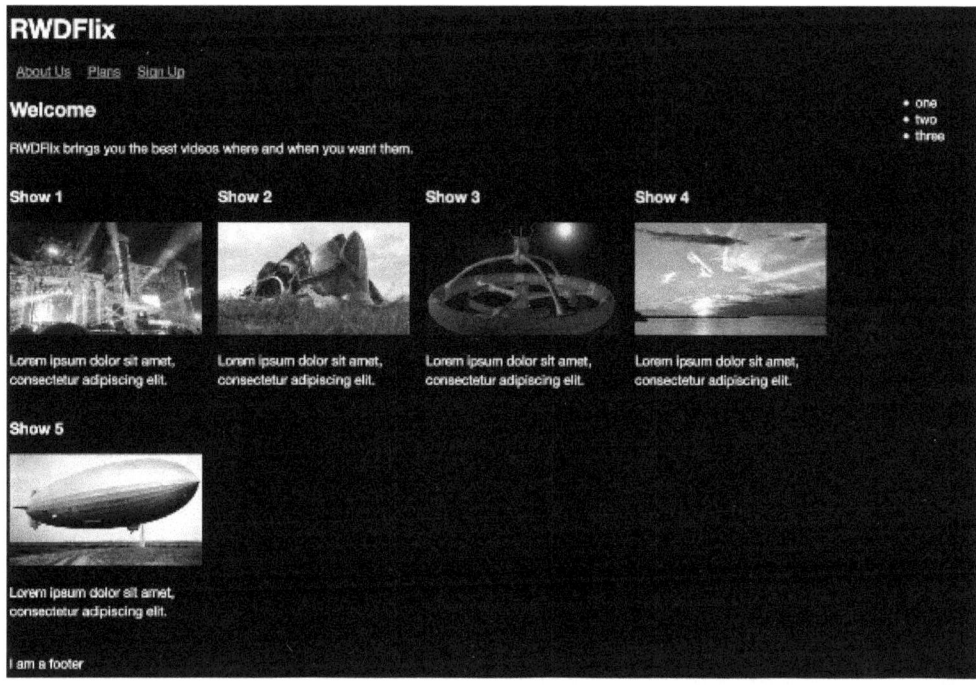

1-5. Final desktop example

Tablet Version

The layout for tablets will focus on allowing users to find a show easily, and, network permitting, to watch it. It will display large thumbnails, the title of the show, the length of the show, the estimated file size, and a description of the show. It will offer to play the video if the user has a data connection or to add the video to a watch list if there's no connection.

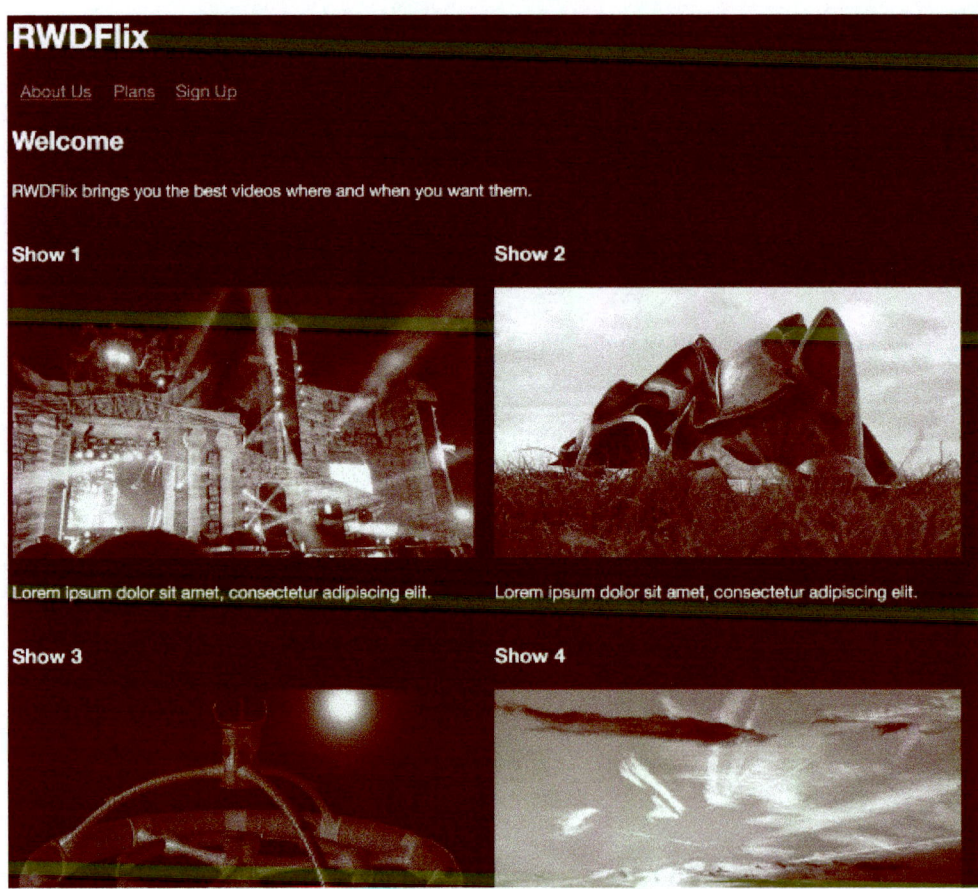

1-6. Final tablet example

Mobile Version

The mobile version will focus on allowing users to find a show easily, and, network permitting, to watch it. It will display smaller thumbnails, the title of the show, the length of the show, and an estimated file size. As with the tablet version, it will offer to play the video if there's a data connection, or add it to a watch list if there's not.

The Meaning and Purpose of Responsive Web Design | 13

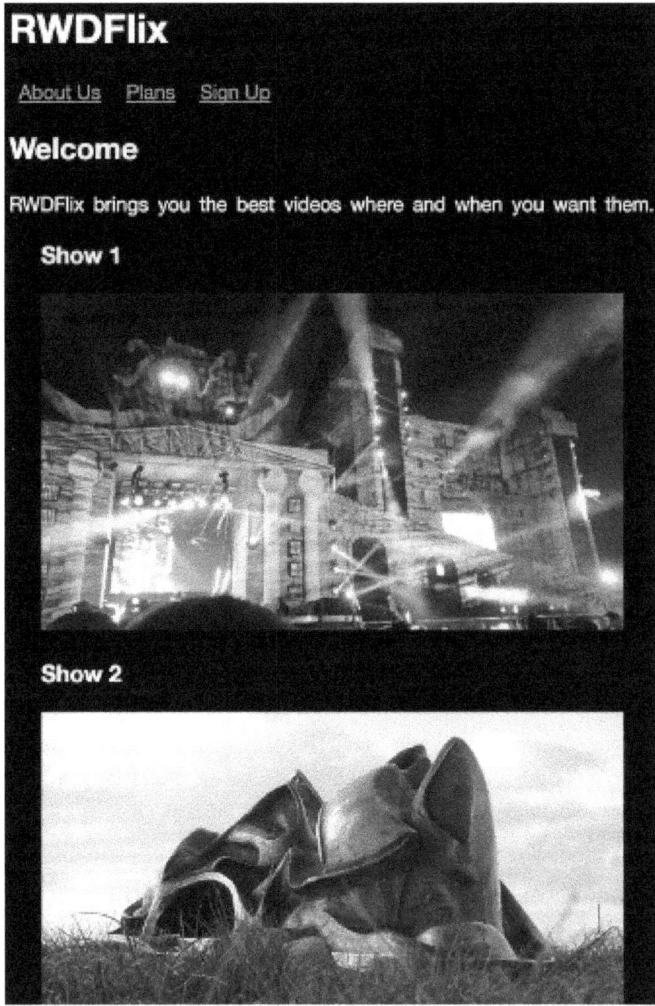

1-7. Final phone example

TV Version

The layout for TVs will display large thumbnails, a video player, a title of the program, the length of the video, and a description of the show. To allow for distance viewing and use, the interface will be large and obvious. While out of the scope of this book, it's also possible that the interface may be controlled and navigated by a physical remote or remote app.

1-8. Final TV example

Structuring a Page with HTML5

Before we get started creating responsive designs and using CSS to implement them, it's important to understand the underlying HTML structure that you'll be manipulating. Recent developments with HTML have made changes to concepts and page structure, so it's useful to recap the tools and options now available to a modern web designer.

Before HTML5, logical sections of HTML pages were structured and organized using generic elements like `divs` and `spans`. These worked fine for many years, but were too broad and didn't help designers or web browsers understand increasingly complex page structures.

Among other things[5], HTML5 introduced new, more semantic elements that describe their use more fully than a simple `div`. The aim of these new elements was to help with things like accessibility and multi-purposing content, but they also help with responsive web design. They include definitions such as the header, navigation or main content area of the page, as well as specific elements for video and audio. Responsive web design is fundamentally about manipulating page layouts to suit different use cases, and better organization and structure of pages helps you target the elements you need to with CSS and media queries (covered in Chapter 2).

---

[5]. https://developer.mozilla.org/en-US/docs/Web/Guide/HTML/HTML5

Let's look at a simplified version of the desktop site. It's a stripped back copy we'll start working with in the next chapter:

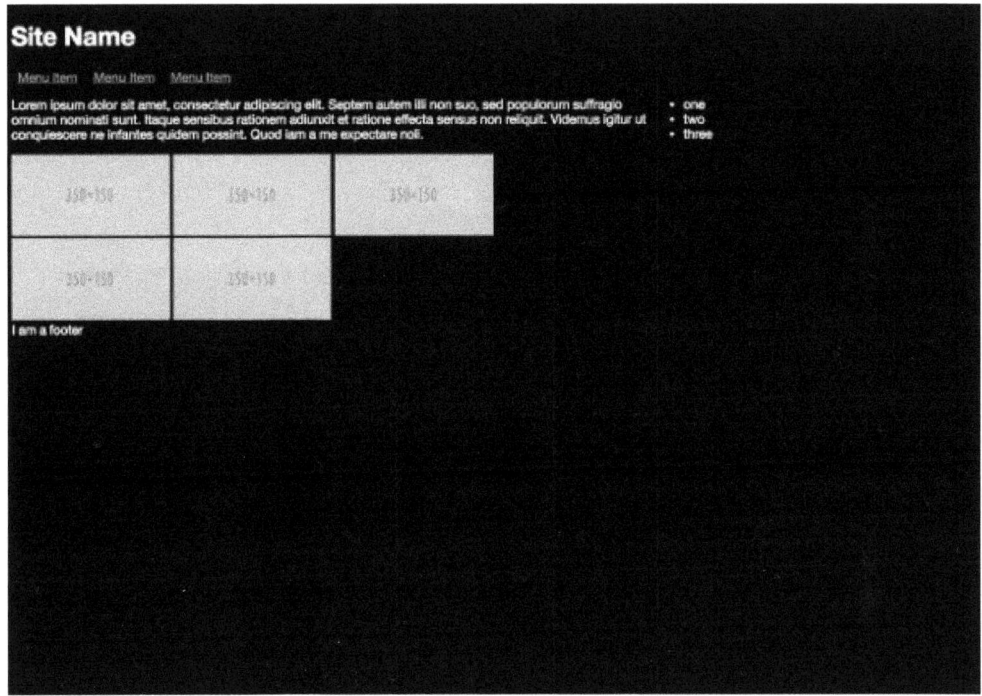

1-9. The current desktop version of the site

And the code:

```
<body>
<header><h1>Site Name</h1></header>

<nav>…</nav>

<main>
    <section>…</section>
    <aside>…</aside>
</main>

<footer>…</footer>

</body>
```

```
</html>
```

Here's where the HTML elements are on the page:

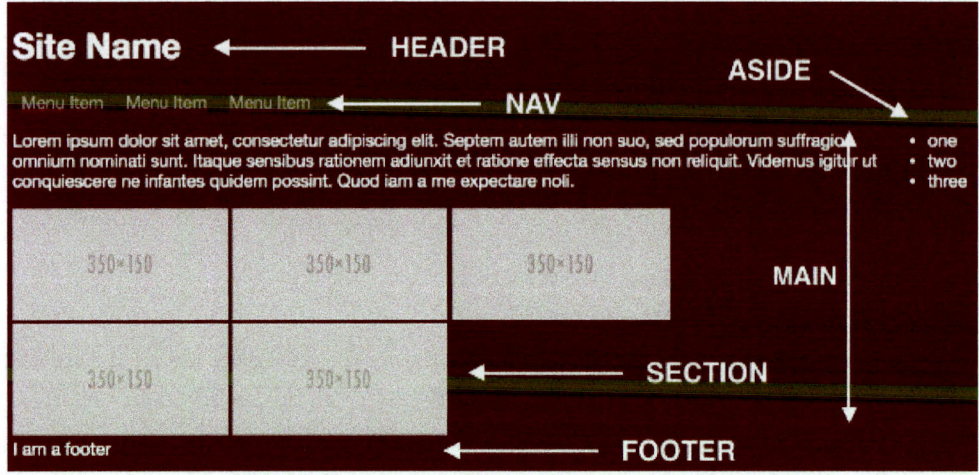

1-10. Marking the individual areas of the page

Here are the functions they perform:

- A `header` element is used for the site name, logo etc. Other sections of the page can also have their own `header` element.
- A `nav` element is used for navigation links, such as a top, side or footer menu.
- A `section` element is used to contain the main content of an article or a significant area of a page.
- An `aside` element defines a small sub-section that relates to a main section.
- A `main` element wraps other elements unique to the page. In our example, these are the `section` and `aside` elements. The other elements will repeat across other pages.
- A `footer` element is used for the site's legal name, dates etc. Other sections of the page can also have their own `footer` element.

The HTML5 specification lists other semantic elements that perform specific functions, and we'll cover many of them in this book. A well-structured page is very important for responsive design, and also helps with accessibility and SEO.

Here's more page content organized in a semantic way:

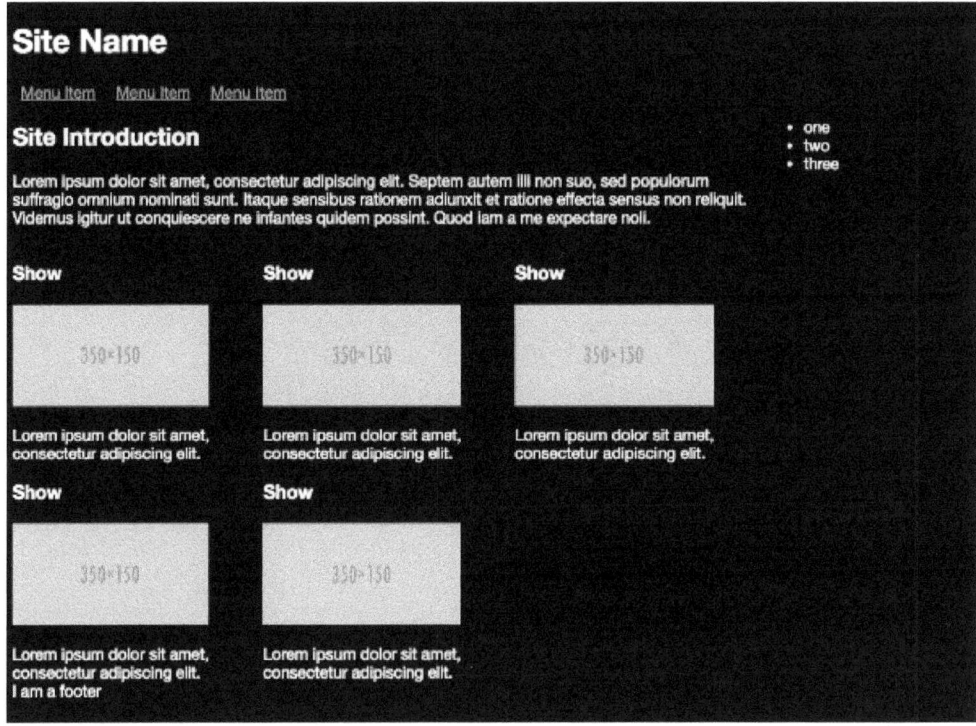

1-11. The TV Shows page

First, I've added a heading for the page, which is an `h2`, as it's the second-level heading on the page, after the main site title which is an `h1`.

Each individual TV show is in its own `section`, under another heading (but an `h3` this time, as it's a level down from the `h2`), along with an image and short description.

1-12. Marking the individual parts of a Show section

1-13. Base/index.html

```
<section class="left">
    <h3>Show</h3>
    <img src="http://placehold.it/350x150"
    class="thumbnail">
    <p>Lorem ipsum dolor sit amet, consectetur
    adipiscing elit.</p>
</section>
```

A typical modern application consists of a back end (which stores the data) and one or more applications that display or consume that data. They include responsive web pages, native mobile apps, and other back-end systems. As you'll see throughout this book, not all contexts will use or display all available data, but instead just the data most relevant to their use case. For example, a TV show episode might have the following values stored in a back end:

- episode name
- series
- length
- age rating
- file size
- show title
- year
- country of origin

- description
- tags
- categories

But the mobile version of the site will only display the values most relevant to a user on a mobile device, ignoring other values only relevant in a different context:

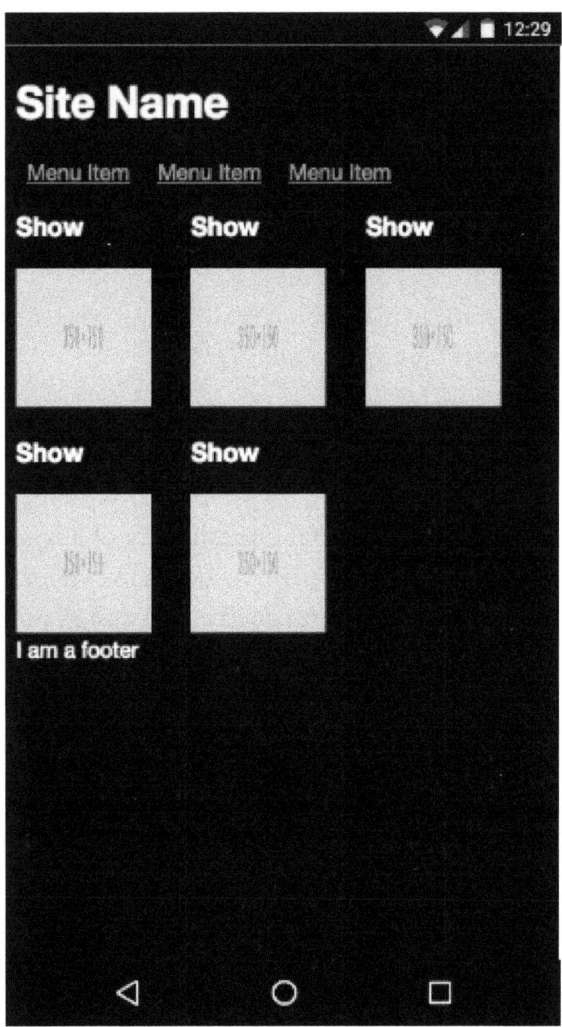

1-14. Mobile version of site

```
<section class="left">
    <h3>Show</h3>
```

```
    <img src="http://placehold.it/125x150"
    class="thumbnail">
</section>
```

The `aside` is for supplemental information, such as contacting support and account information. The mobile version of the site is optimized for browsing and watching videos, so the `aside` isn't displayed. This layout isn't the only possibility, of course. You could, for example, choose to display the `aside` at the bottom of the screen (which we'll cover when looking at grid systems).

As the screen size decreases, the TV show descriptions get increasingly curtailed to bring more attention to the thumbnails, which are resized appropriately for a mobile device.

If you're interested in learning more about HTML5 and page structure, I recommend you read SitePoint's *Jump Start HTML5*[6].

Ready to Respond?

In this chapter, I've looked at the need for, and history of, responsive design. I've covered the sorts of devices your website now needs to support, and introduced the demo site I'll use to demonstrate responsive web design principles throughout the rest of the book. We also took a brief look at structuring a page with HTML5. Now we're ready to dig into the building blocks of responsive design, which is the focus of the following chapter.

---

[6]. https://www.sitepoint.com/premium/books/jump-start-html5

Chapter 2

The Building Blocks of Responsive Design

There are two main building blocks at the heart of responsive web design: media queries and viewports.

Media queries represent the glue that joins a lot of other responsive concepts and tools together. They're a simple but powerful concept, allowing you to detect device properties, define rules, and load different CSS properties based on them. For example, you can optimize a navigation menu for different devices, converting a full horizontal menu on desktop browsers to the "hamburger" menu often encountered on mobile devices.

Viewports are less complex, allowing you to define the size and scaling factor of a web page appropriately, no matter what the size of the device being used to view the page is. Without them, media queries would only be partially useful.

This chapter will introduce media queries first, and then show how you can make them work better for you by defining a viewport.

Media Types

You can invoke media query dependent styles in several ways, most commonly with the HTML `link` element linking to one or more CSS files, or from directly within a CSS file with `@import`.

In HTML, this example will load the `style.css` file if the query is true, which it will be on all device types:

```
<link rel="stylesheet" media="all" href="/style.css">
```

In the following example, `@import` does the same, but from within a CSS file:

```
@import url("/style.css") all;
```

In the example below, the `@media` CSS rule contains a specific set of selectors that will load if the query is true:

```
@media all {
    ...
}
```

The `all` in these queries is the **media type**. There are four media types available (at the time of writing):

- `print`: for print versions of pages
- `screen`: for computer, tablet and phone screens
- `speech`: for screen readers that read pages to the user
- `all`: for all of the above

Adding a media type allows you to specify what types of devices the query applies to. These are broad and don't allow for a lot of control. To target devices more specifically, you add expressions to these media types.

Creating a Query

Let's try something more useful. The `aside` to the main content in RWDflix is designed to show announcements and news. Mobile and tablet visitors probably want to focus on watching shows and nothing else, so let's hide this element for users of smaller screened devices.

 Method Used in This Book

> For the remainder of this chapter, I'll use the `@media` method shown above for media queries. It's a personal preference, and as an experiment, you might like to try re-writing the examples using other methods.

Remove the current `aside` CSS class and replace it with the following media queries:

```
@media screen and (min-width: 680px) {
    aside {
        width: 33%;
    }
}

@media screen and (max-width: 680px) {
    aside {
        display: none;
    }
}
```

This pair of media queries sets the `aside` element to a width of 33% if the screen is wider than 680px (by asking if the screen is *at least* 680px wide with `min-width`), and hides it if the screen is narrower than 680px (asking if the screen is *at most* 680px wide with `max-width`).

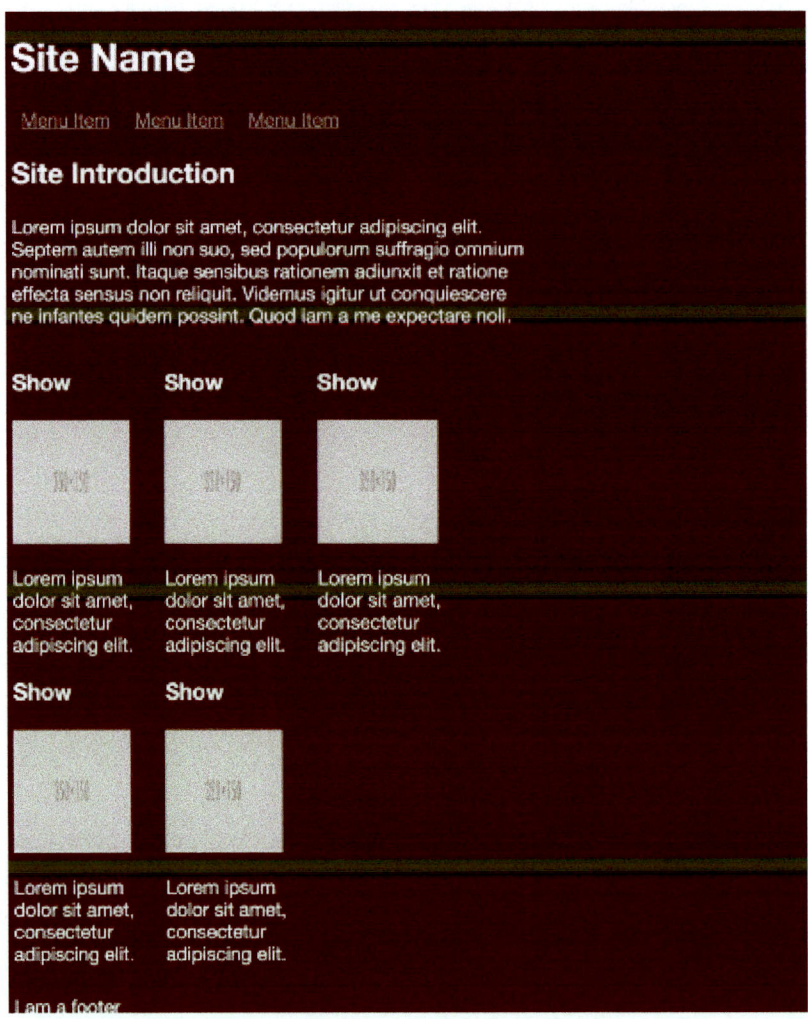

2-1. The `aside` element hidden on smaller screens

Next, make the TV listings fill the screen width when the `aside` isn't showing:

```
section.showslisting {
    margin-bottom: 25px;
}

@media screen and (min-width: 680px) {
    section.showslisting {
        width: 66%;
    }
```

```
}

@media screen and (max-width: 680px) {
    section.showslisting {
        width: 100%;
    }
}
```

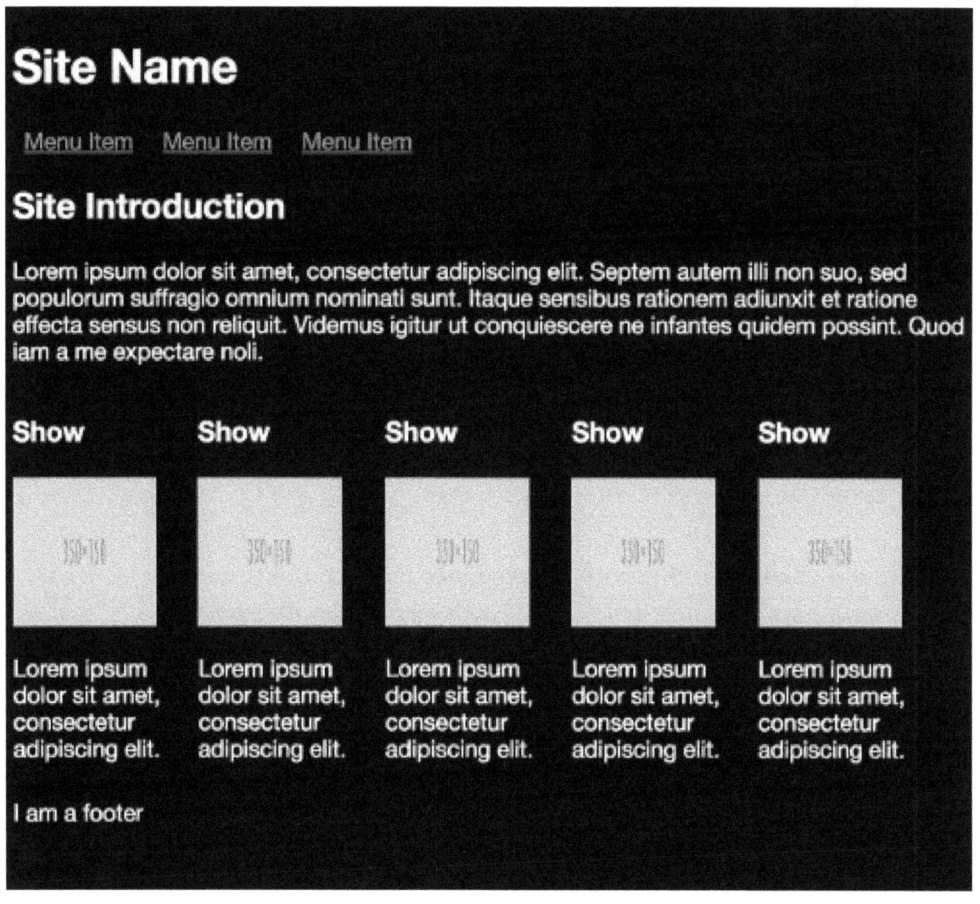

2-2. The main content now set to full width

If you resize the page in your desktop browser, you'll see the `aside` appearing and disappearing as you widen and narrow the browser window, the main content adjusting appropriately.

You can use basic logic in your media queries. This allows you to combine multiple conditions. For example, you can use a logical AND:

```
@media only screen and (min-width: 640px) and (max-width:
↪ 1136px) {
    ...
}
```

The code above will invoke the CSS styles within the query if a device's screen width is between 640px *and* 1136px. The `min-width` property is the minimum width of the screen, and `max-width` the maximum.

For this media query to match, both conditions need to be true. It's also possible to match queries if only one condition is true with a logical OR, which (confusingly) is represented with a comma. The query below will apply on `screen` or `print` devices:

```
@media only screen, print {
    ...
}
```

You can also combine ANDs with ORs to make more complex queries. Here's the current page rendered on a larger sized phone, but in landscape mode:

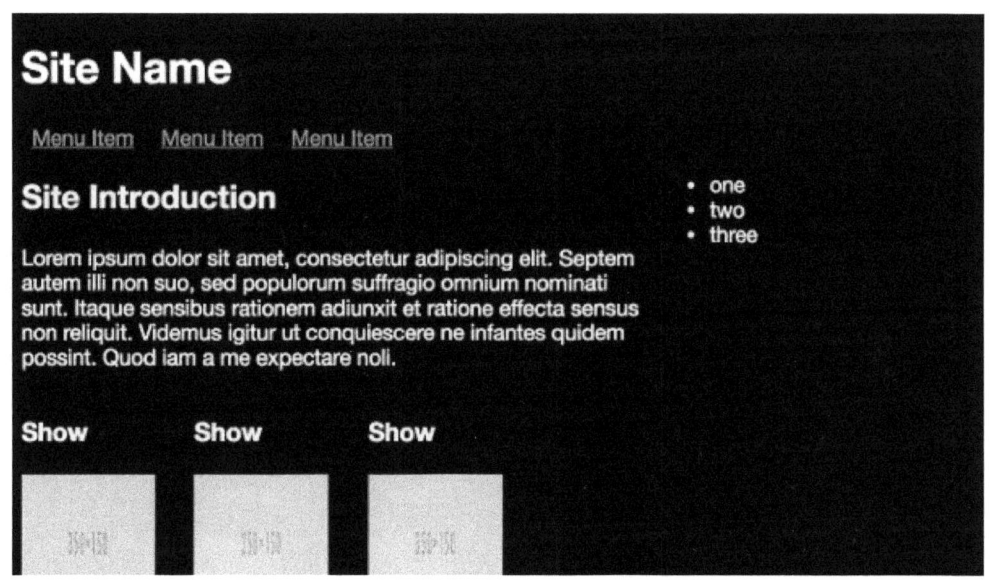

2-3. The current phone layout in landscape mode

In the screenshot above, the screen is 732px wide, which is above the 640px set above. Still, the `aside` doesn't quite fit into the window, so let's hide it if the screen size is below 640px, or if the device is in landscape mode:

```
@media screen and (max-width: 680px), screen and
↪ (orientation: landscape) and (max-width: 750px) {
    aside {
        display: none;
    }
}
```

And the corresponding media query for the listings section:

```
@media screen and (max-width: 680px), screen and
↪ (orientation: landscape) and (max-width: 750px) {
    section.showslisting {
        width: 100%;
    }
}
```

You'll see that I added a `max-width` check, to show the `aside` on tablets in landscape mode, but also to show how you can combine logical checks together.

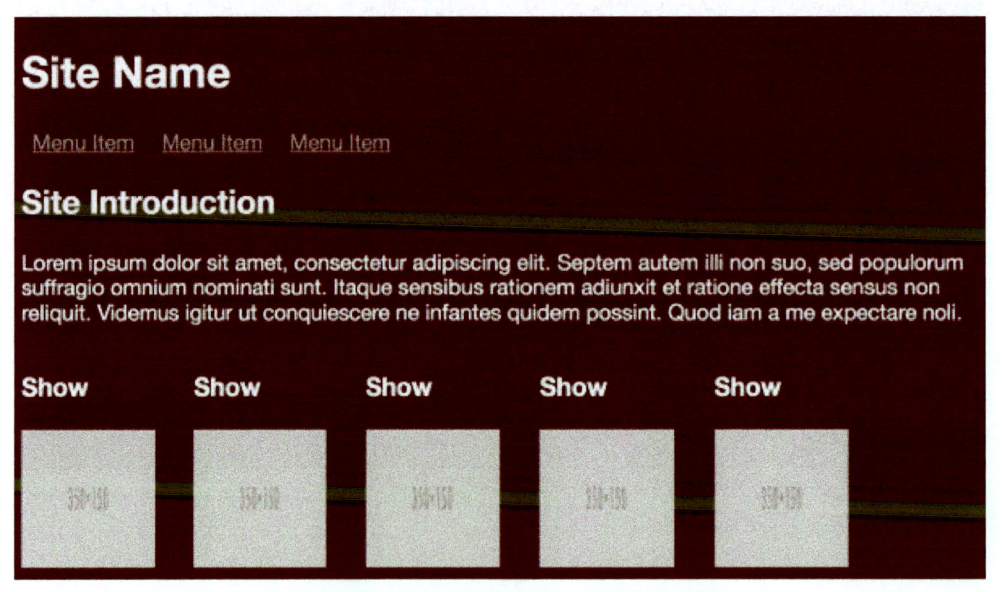

2-4. The aside removed from landscape device orientation

Logical Queries with Only and Not

You can also make precise media queries using `only` and `not`. For example, this media query will match devices that are at least `640px` wide and *exclude* the print media type:

```
@media not print and (min-width: 640px) {
    ...
}
```

In contrast, this query will *only* apply to screen devices that are at least `640px` wide:

```
@media only screen and (min-width: 640px) {
    ...
}
```

Query Features

The `width` and `height` queries we've looked at so far are some of the most widely used, but there are several other **media features** that are also useful for checking against device features. These include color capabilities, aspect ratio, orientation, resolution, and vendor-specific features for Mozilla- and WebKit-based browsers. Most of these accept `min-` and `max-` prefixes that work in a similar way to the dimension queries above.

`aspect-ratio`

The `aspect-ratio` feature allows you to check the ratio of horizontal pixels to vertical pixels, separated by a slash. For example:

```
@media screen and (min-aspect-ratio: 1/1) {
    ...
}
```

The above rule will match a device where the screen's width to height ratio is 1:1 or more, so square or landscape.

A common use for this would be to detect wider screens, useful when you're displaying videos:

```
@media screen and (min-aspect-ratio: 16/9) {
    ...
}
```

`orientation`

As shown earlier, this feature checks if the device is in landscape or portrait mode. For example:

```css
@media all and (orientation: landscape) {
    ...
}
```

And:

```css
@media all and (orientation: portrait) {
    ...
}
```

`color`

This feature checks if a device can support a certain bit-level of color. For example, this is how to check that a device supports at least 8-bits of color (that is, 256 colors):

```css
@media all and (min-color: 8) {
    ...
}
```

`color-index`

This plays a role similar to `color`, but lets you check for the number of colors instead of the bit-level:

```css
@media all and (min-color-index: 256) {
    ...
}
```

monochrome

Again, similar to `color`, `monochrome` lets you check for the levels of gray in a device:

```
@media all and (min-monochrome: 8) {
    ...
}
```

resolution

This feature targets devices that have high-resolution screens:

```
@media all and (min-resolution: 120dpi) {
    ...
}
```

scan

The `scan` media feature lets you check the scanning process of TVs, the options being `interlace` or `progressive`:

```
@media all and (scan: progressive) {
    ...
}
```

grid

`grid` is used for checking if a device is a terminal-like device. This also includes older phones (that is, non-smartphones), accessible phones (for those with poor vision), and braille devices. It returns a boolean value if true:

```
@media grid {
    ...
}
```

As you can see, through combinations of dimension- and feature-based queries, you can construct complex stylesheets to target a multitude of devices effectively with styles that work most efficiently for them. This is the main point of media queries: they allow you to selectively load CSS styles for particular device configurations.

Streamlining the Example App

Now that you have a basic understanding, let's continue to build upon the media queries added earlier to make the example site tidier.

First, you can consolidate the queries already written, moving the classes into two groups of media queries:

```
/* Media Queries */
/* For example, desktop devices */
@media screen and (min-width: 680px) {
    aside {
        width: 33%;
    }

    section.showslisting {
        width: 66%;
    }
}

 /* For example, medium-width screens or smaller screens in
↪ landscape */
 @media screen and (max-width: 680px), screen and
↪ (orientation: landscape) and (max-width: 750px) {
    aside {
        display: none;
    }
```

```
    section.showslisting {
        width: 100%;
    }
}
```

Much tidier! You can keep adding new styles for each query into these sections.

Let's look back to our demo site specification outlined in Chapter 1 for what else needs to be optimized for each screen size. The next step will be hiding the TV show description on small screens, and shorten it on medium-sized screens.

It would be a lot easier to do this if the description text had a class, so add one to each instance of the `p` tag that contains the show description:

```
<section class="tvshow">
    <h3>Show</h3>
    <img src="http://placehold.it/350x150"
    class="thumbnail">
    <p class="showdescription">Lorem ipsum dolor sit amet,
    consectetur adipiscing elit.</p>
</section>
```

Let's add new media queries to accommodate the various sizes we aim to support, and, in doing so, tidy up the existing ones.

The specific widths at which we want our design to reflow are known as **breakpoints**. The breakpoints we'll add are not exhaustive: there's a huge range of device sizes, and more are appearing all the time, so it's futile to try to target each device with separate queries. A better approach is to assess the points at which your design needs to reflow, and then create media queries for those breakpoints. This is the beauty of responsive web design: you can ensure that each device will get an appropriate layout without having to design separately for each device.

Add the following breakpoints and refactor our existing styles into them:

2-5. Chapter2/demo_create/layout.css *(excerpt)*

```css
/* Media Queries */

/* For example, older phones */
@media only screen and (min-width: 320px) {
    aside {
        display: none;
    }

    section.showslisting {
        width: 100%;
    }

    .showdescription {
        display: none;
    }
}

/* For example, newer phones */
@media only screen and (min-width: 480px) {
}

/* For example, small computer screens and larger tablets */
@media only screen and (min-width: 768px) {
    .showdescription {
        text-overflow: ellipsis;
        display: block;
        white-space: nowrap;
        width: 100px;
        overflow: hidden;
    }
}

 /* For example, typical desktop monitors or larger tablet
↪ devices */
@media only screen and (min-width: 992px) {
    aside {
        width: 33%;
        display: block;
    }
```

```
    section.showslisting {
        width: 66%;
    }

    .showdescription {
        white-space: normal;
        width: 125px;
    }
}

/* Large Devices, for example large monitors and TVs */
@media only screen and (min-width: 1200px) {
}
```

The media queries should now be self-explanatory. They define queries for a selection of devices, defined using screen sizes. As the C in CSS implies, the media queries **cascade**: you can build upon styles defined in a breakpoint for a smaller device size and change the properties that are different.

Notice that between the `@media only screen and (min-width: 320px)` breakpoint for smaller devices and the `@media only screen and (min-width: 768px)` breakpoint for medium-sized devices, all that changes is the `showdescription` class, showing text, but truncating it. Then in the `@media only screen and (min-width: 992px)` breakpoint for larger screens, all elements are revealed.

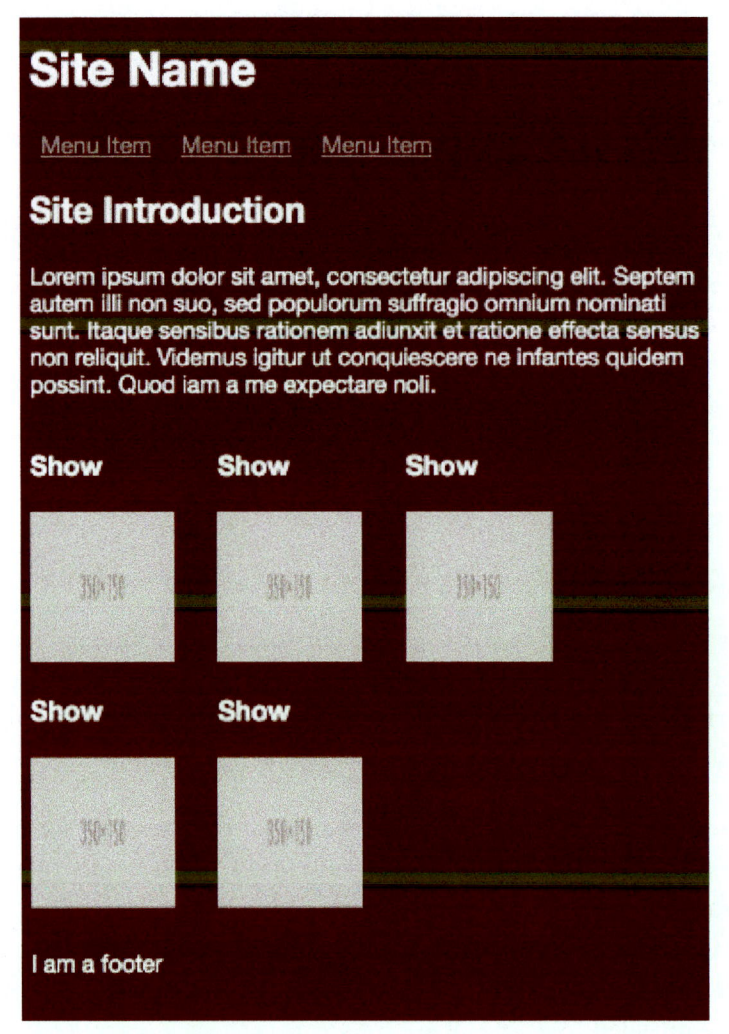

2-6. The layout generated by the small-screen breakpoint

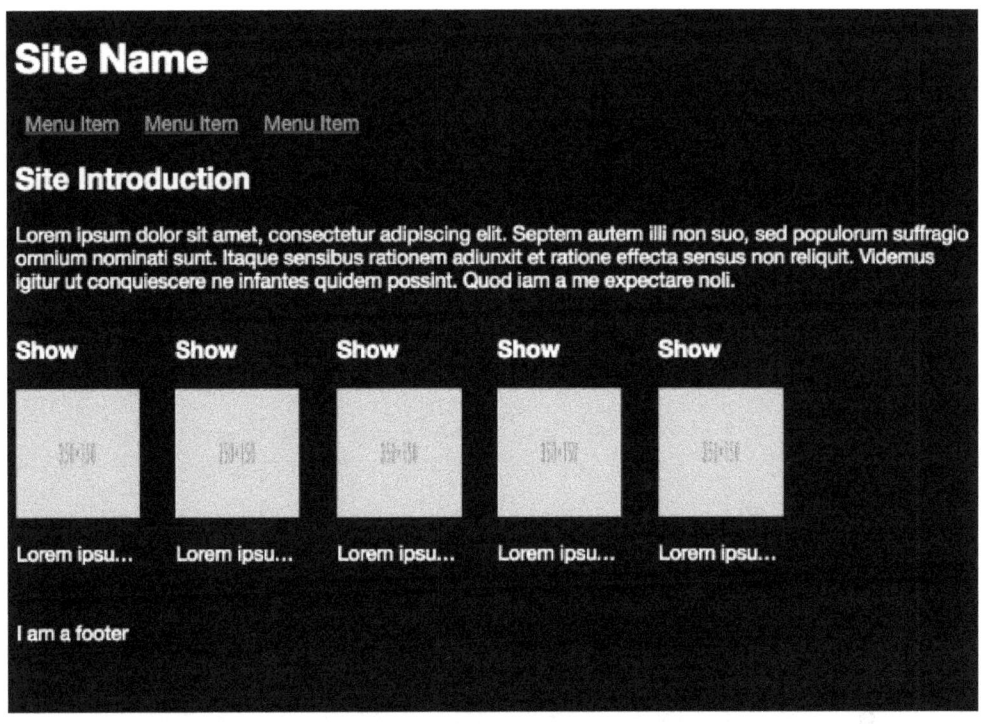

2-7. The layout generated by the medium breakpoint

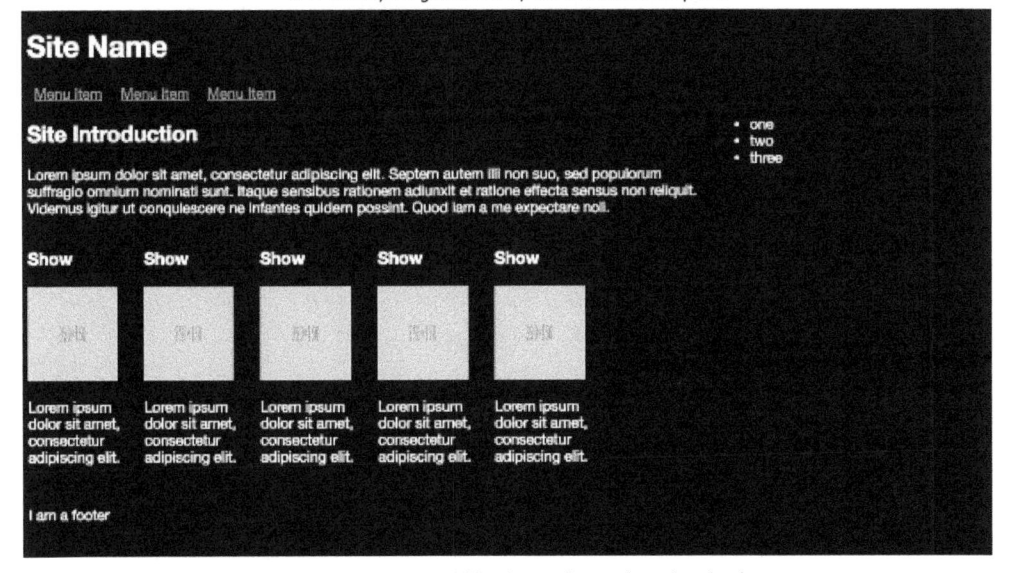

2-8. The layout generated by the medium to large breakpoint

Mobile First

In Chapter 1, I introduced the "mobile first" concept. Currently, the page works on different device sizes but is not mobile first, because the "default" styles—that is, those not inside media queries—are really designed for larger devices. So let's do some rearranging and refactoring to make the design mobile first. This won't involve too much work.

Make the following changes to the classes outside of the media queries:

```css
aside {
    display: none;
}

section.showslisting {
    margin-bottom: 25px;
    width: 100%;
}

.showdescription {
    display: none;
}
```

You can now remove the corresponding classes from inside the `@media only screen and (min-width: 320px)` media query.

That's it! In essence, all "mobile first" means is to make the default styles relevant to mobile devices and older browsers that don't support media queries and add more specific styles (via media queries) from there.

There's another, more hidden advantage to the mobile first approach. While all modern browsers now support media queries, some older versions (Internet Explorer 8, for example) don't, and in this case, the default CSS styles will still be loaded.

The Viewport Meta Element

In the last section, I covered making the demo page mobile first with media queries. If you try the example in your desktop browser and resize the window, everything looks as you would expect. But if you try it in a mobile browser, or with an emulated mobile browser, you'll probably see something like the screenshot below and be disappointed. Aren't media queries supposed to make pages better in a mobile browser?

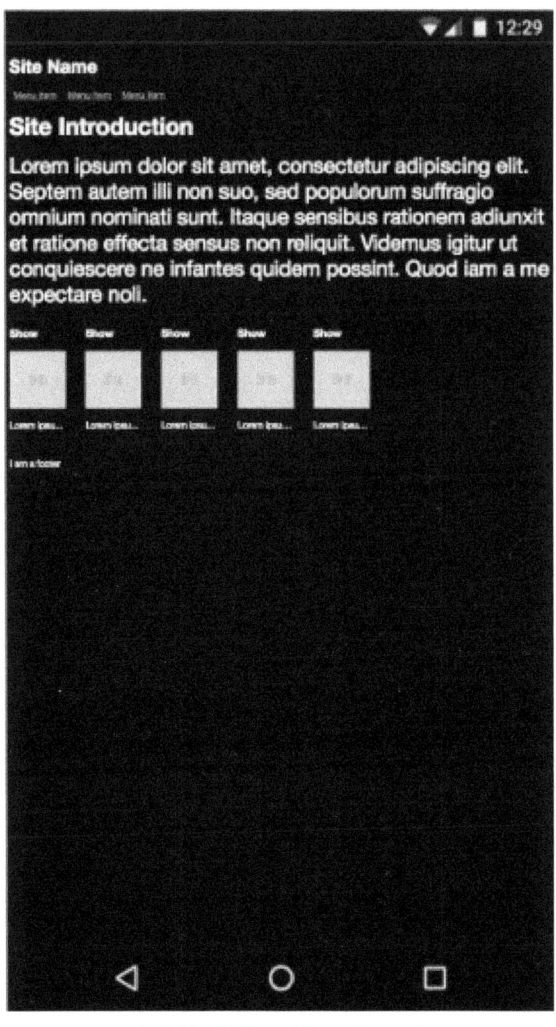

2-9. Mobile first with no viewport

Media queries allow us to set different styles for different screen sizes. So, if your desktop browser's viewport is 1200px wide, any media query styles targeting that screen width will apply. If you're on a mobile device with a viewport width of 320px, you'd expect that any styles targeting a 320px wide viewport would kick into action. But there's a very big catch. By default, many devices, such as mobile phones and tablets, act as if they have a wider screen than they really do.

To explain what's going on here, let's look at the iPhone, where this behavior originated. The first iPhone had a screen/viewport width of 320px. However, most websites designed for desktops were much wider than that. To avoid only seeing the top left corner of these sites on initial load, Apple developed the concept of a "virtual viewport" or "layout viewport". Websites were loaded onto this much wider viewport, which was then scaled down to fit on the screen. So most sites got rendered on iPhones with tiny text that you had to zoom to be able to read.

Apple's virtual viewport was set at 980px, so as long as a website was no wider than that, the whole layout would appear on screen. Any layouts wider than 980px would still be partly hidden off to the right, requiring sideways scrolling. And that's still the case today. The virtual viewport idea has been adopted by other device makers as well, though the default width varies.

When designing a responsive site, we really don't want this default behavior on mobile devices. We want to know that the canvas we're working with is the actual screen area of each device. Fortunately, there's a simple way to tell these devices not to behave in the default way. All we need to do is add a special meta element to the head of each page. Here's a typical example:

```
<meta name="viewport" content="width=device-width,
↪ initial-scale=1">
```

As a general rule, the line above is all you need to ensure your media queries do what you expect on mobile devices. The name attribute specifies that we're targeting the virtual viewport, and the content attribute specifies how we want the device to behave. In the example above, we're specifying that the virtual viewport should match the actual width of the screen, and that there should be no zoom applied to the content.

With the viewport declaration in place, you can be sure that media queries targeting a device that's 320px wide will actually be recognized by that device.

Let's modify our demo site to add a viewport declaration. Add the following `meta` tag inside your current `head` element:

2-10. Chapter2/demo_viewport/index.html *(excerpt)*

```
<head>
    <meta charset="UTF-8">
    <title>App Name</title>
    <link rel="stylesheet" type="text/css" media="all"
    href="layout.css">
    <meta name="viewport" content="width=device-width,
    initial-scale=1.0">
</head>
```

Refresh the page:

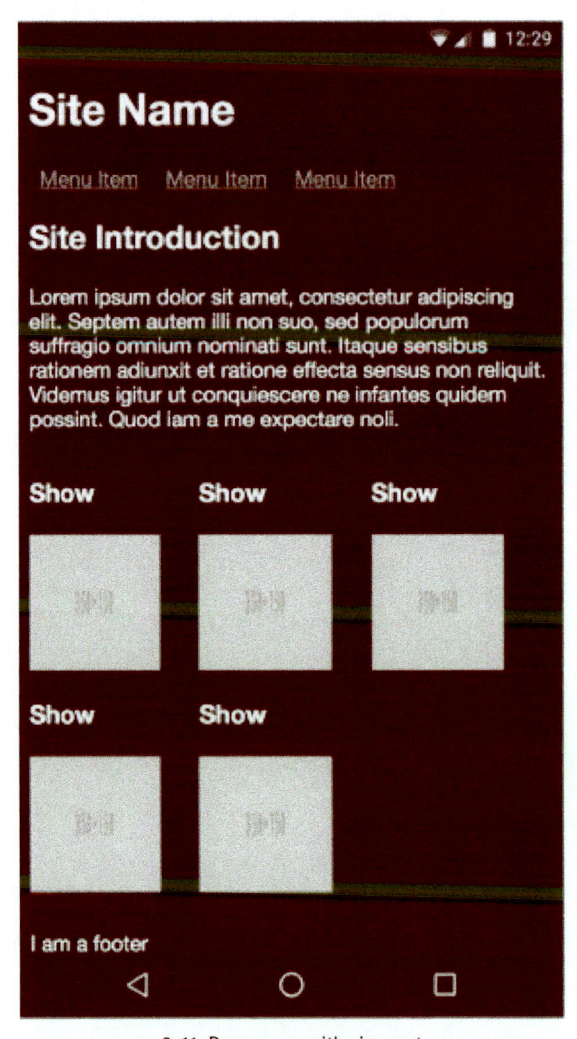

2-11. Demo page with viewport

Much better!

The Viewport

Viewport is an old term in computer graphics to define the (typically rectangular) screen area used to render the elements that users see in a browser. When web browsing was limited to desktop browsers, the viewport still existed but was rarely changed by designers. With the increasing variety of browser dimensions, HTML5 introduced a `viewport` attribute to the `meta` element that allowed designers to set and manipulate this area.

The viewport meta element was initially proposed by Apple to set the initial state of the page to the correct size and was later introduced as part of the HTML5 standard.

Generally, you set the viewport to the width of the current device (with `width=device-width`) and leave the content unscaled (with `initial-scale=1.0`).

The `width` attribute is a pixel value, and the `device-width` constant detects the current device width, meaning you don't need to handle the myriad sizes that may be available; the meta element will take care of it for you. The same applies for different screen orientations: changes between landscape and portrait are also handled for you. There's still a lot more work needed to make a design fully responsive, but media queries plus this viewport setting give you a fantastic start.

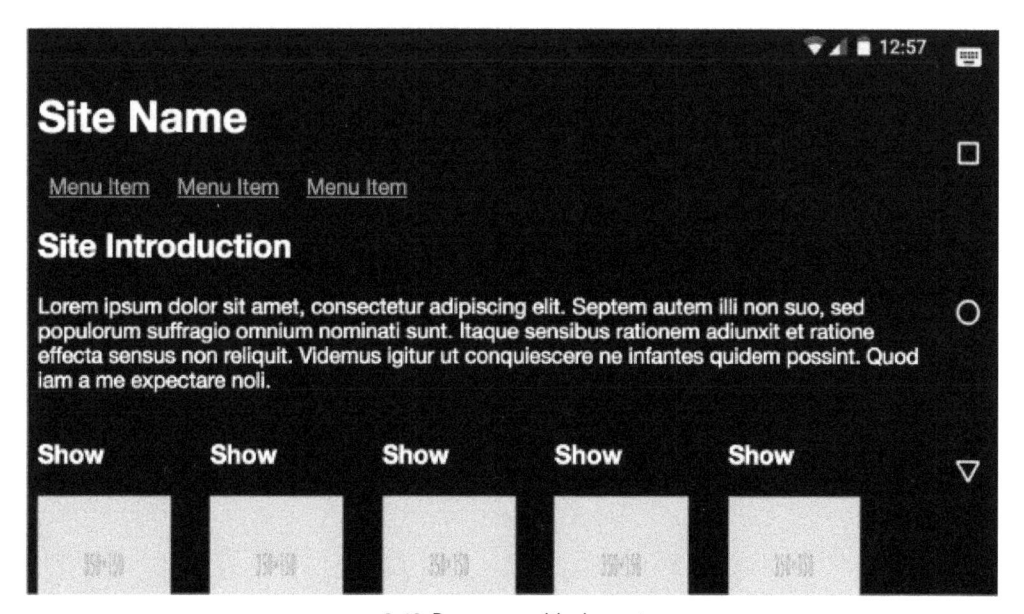

2-12. Demo page with viewport

The `content` attribute of the tag also accepts standard methods for setting the width. For example:

```
<head>
    ...
    <meta name="viewport" content="width=500,
    initial-scale=1.0">
    ...
</head>
```

Which will result in:

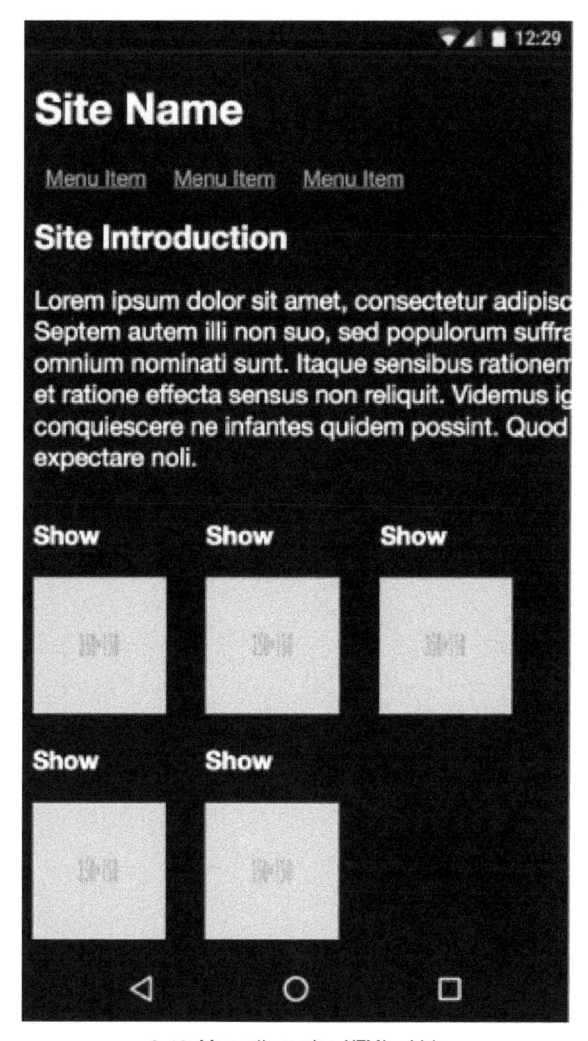

2-13. Manually setting HTML width

This is still a better result than a page without the viewport, but as you can see, if the page content is wider than the width you define, it will continue anyway. One use case for setting a manual width is if you're certain of screen dimensions, and certain that your page content will fit perfectly—for example, if you're only targeting one device, like an eReader, or kiosk application.

There are other, less frequently used attributes for the viewport meta element that have limited use, but which you might need for more fine-grained control over your page layout:

- `minimum-scale`: the minimum zoom level, or how much the user can zoom out.
- `maximum-scale`: the maximum zoom level, or how much the user can zoom in.
- `user-scalable=no`: disables zooming. While this has a limited number of use cases[1], it significantly reduces the accessibility of your page.

Any Queries?

The selective nature of media queries makes them an essential tool in your responsive toolbox, and in this chapter, we've learned how to create and use them.

Every modern browser now supports them, and they offer the potential to target any specific environments you need to design for.

In coming chapters, we'll leverage the responsive foundation that media queries and the viewport offer to add polish and shine to our responsive designs.

---

[1]. https://codepen.io/absolutholz/post/user-scalable-no-evil-or-slightly-not-evil

Chapter 3

Better Responsive Structures with Grid Systems

So far, we've looked at the underlying principles of responsive design and the power of media queries to build page structures optimized for different devices. In this chapter, we'll see how grid systems can supplement and even replace some of the techniques we've covered so far, providing more flexibility for how pages display across different devices.

While flexibility in design is endless in theory, a common design ethic in print and digital design has been to use loose horizontal and vertical grids for element layout. They help break up sections of a page into logical areas that are easier to manage, and our brains like to see items in a composition in predictable lines. Composition in artwork and photos is a long-standing field of study, and many of its theories continue into web design.

If you look at the current demo page on a desktop, it's effectively a grid consisting of four rows and two columns:

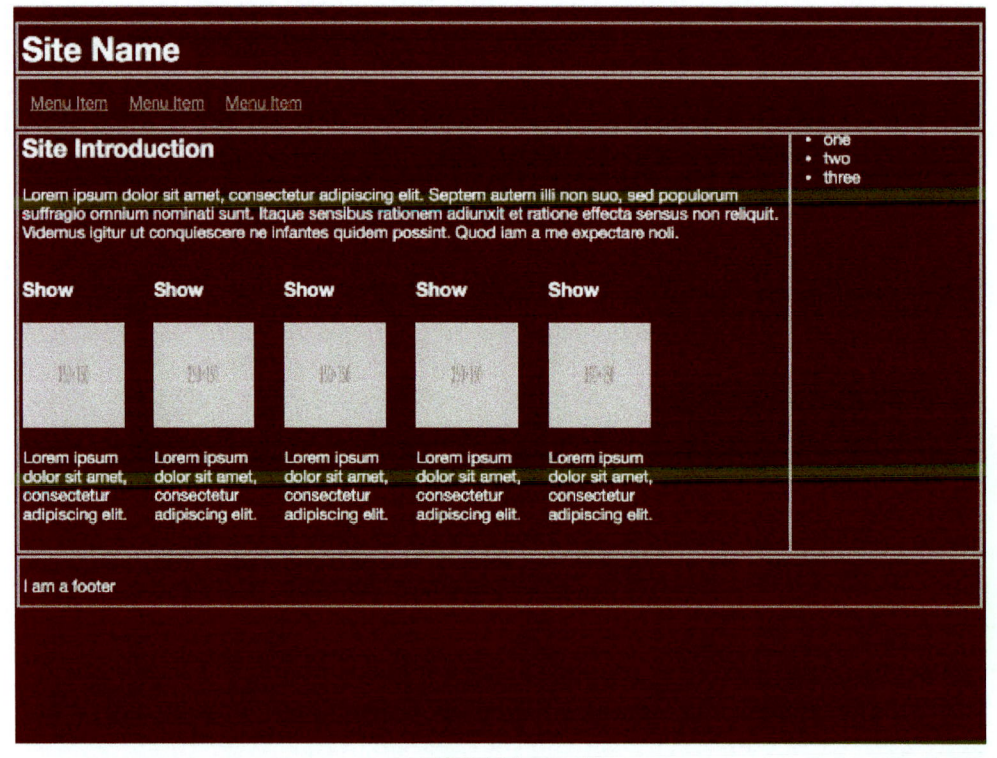

3-1. The initial page grid

When you resize the page, the media queries added in the last chapter take care of changing the row and column layouts to fit accordingly.

This is because the current layout is a simple example of what's called a **fluid grid**. The main sections of the page have widths that are percentages of the viewport width, and thus will resize accordingly.

On a desktop, the main listing of the TV shows takes up 66% (or two thirds) of the web page, and the menu 33% (or one third).

3-2. Chapter3/start/layout.css *(excerpt)*

```css
@media only screen and (min-width: 992px) {
    aside {
        width: 33%;
        display: block;
    }

    section.showslisting {
        width: 66%;
    }

    .showdescription {
        white-space: normal;
        width: 125px;
    }
}
```

The fluidity of the design can go further than this. Layouts inside a page area can also take up a percentage of the available space. For example, you could set the individual TV listings to have a flexible width:

```css
section.tvshow {
    width: 20%;
    height: 150px;
    display: inline-block;
}
```

This means that each subsection will take up 20% of the main content area, no matter what the screen size is. This can start to get fiddly, and is more of an example to show that percentage-based sizes can go anywhere—on text and even media elements (both of which we'll cover in later chapters).

While the current page layout is a grid, it could be better, with more meaningful class names and a better structure.

Create a new `div` element with a class of `container` that wraps all the current content within the `body` element:

3-3. Chapter3/vanilla_final/index.html *(excerpt)*

```html
<body>
<div class="container">
    …
</div>
</body>
```

Add the following styles for this `div` to your stylesheet:

3-4. Chapter3/vanilla_final/layout.css *(excerpt)*

```css
.container {
    width: 95%;
    margin-left: auto;
    margin-right: auto;
    max-width: 1180px;
}
```

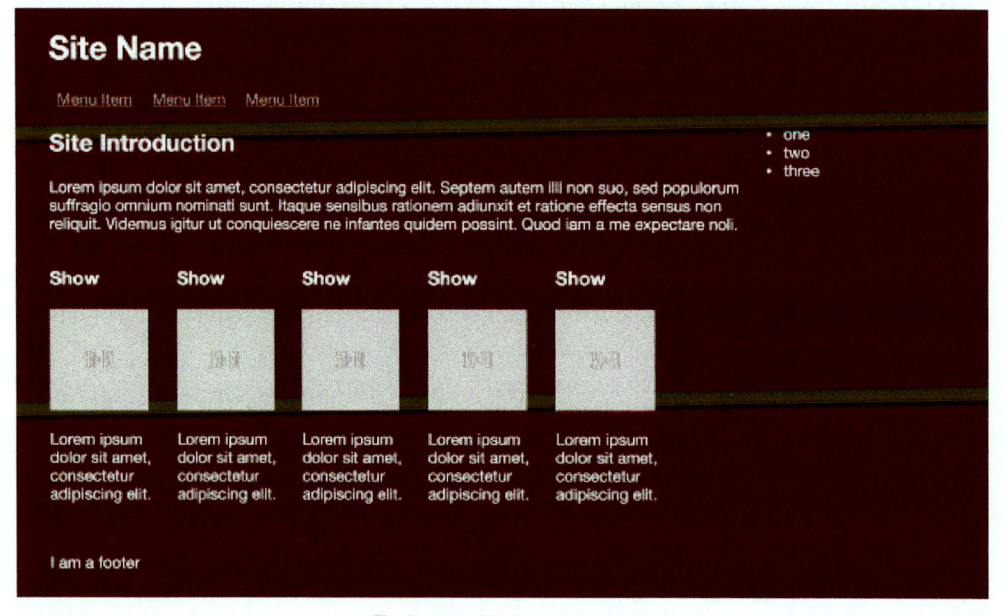

3-5. The layout with the extra container

This is a common way to set up a containing element for page content. It sets a maximum width of 1180px, a width of 95% of the browser window, and centers the container in the window using the handy left and right `auto` margins.

> **Why 1180px?**
>
> Why is the `max-width` set to 1180px? This is an arbitrary value and based upon current trends in desktop screen sizes; it's added to make sure the page doesn't get *too* wide on giant screens. For a long time, it was 960px, reflecting that most screen widths were at most 1024px wide. As screen dimensions and resolutions have grown, this maximum width has become larger, but is still open to different opinions. Media queries (covered in Chapter 2) have made this maximum width less relevant than it used to be. For now, stick with this `1180px` value.

Next, add a `row` class to the header, navigation, listings and footer elements. You can also now remove the `left` class from these elements, as you'll consolidate its CSS properties:

```
<header class="row">
    ...
</header>

<nav class="row">
    ...
</nav>

<main class="row">
    ...
</main>

<footer class="row">
    ...
</footer>
```

And define the `row` CSS class:

```css
.row {
    clear: both;
    float: left;
}
```

This `row` fills the width of the container and floats to the left, meaning that as a browser window resizes, it will flow with it, fixed to the left side. As you haven't yet defined the columns in the rows, the `aside` menu is pushed to the bottom on larger screen sizes.

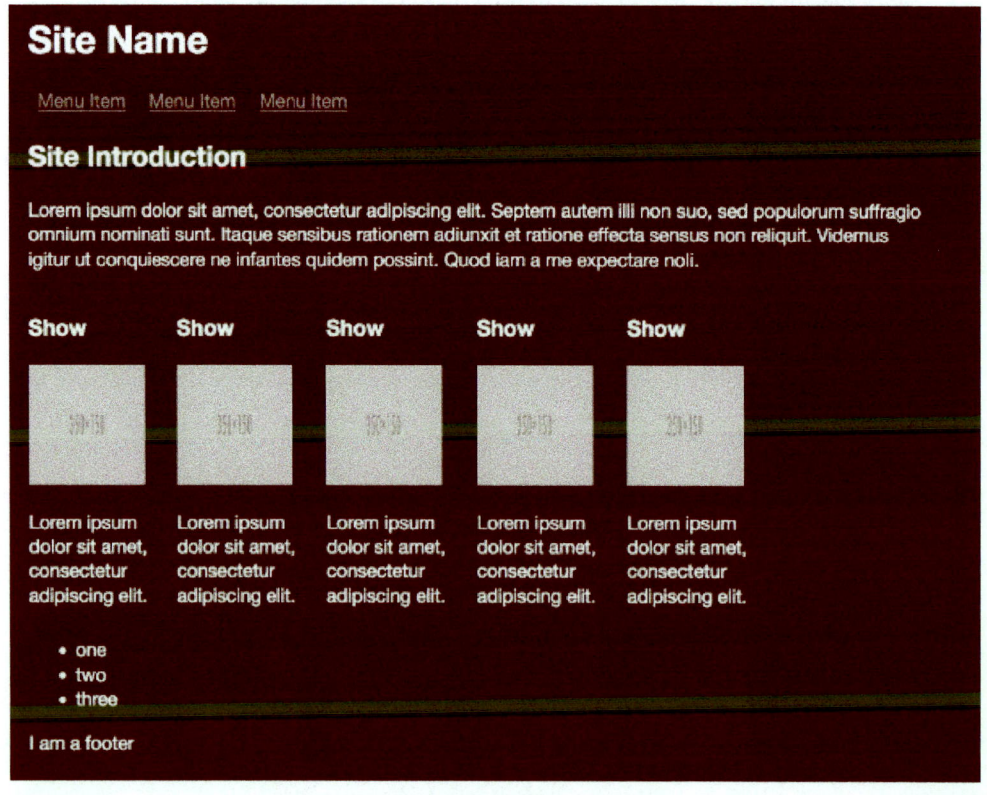

3-6. The new page structure

Now that everything horizontal on the page is in four rows, it's time to define the columns inside the rows. Some of the rows are a single, full-width column, while others are subdivided.

To start afresh, remove the simpler percentage widths set earlier (from all media queries), so that you have the following:

```
@media only screen and (min-width: 320px) {
    aside {
        display: none;
    }

    section.showslisting {
    }

    .showdescription {
        display: none;
    }
}
...
@media only screen and (min-width: 992px) {
    aside {
        display: block;
    }

    section.showslisting {
    }

    .showdescription {
        white-space: normal;
        width: 125px;
    }
}
```

The page is no longer flowing so well at larger screen sizes, but you'll fix this soon.

What Is a Grid?

Before you restructure the page into a fluid grid, let's take a quick aside to discuss what a grid is.

A **grid** is a series of columns and rows. But how many rows and columns do you need for your site? The number of rows is more clear: it's as many as you need to fit your header, navigation, content, footer etc. What about columns? Well, as with other topics in this book (and technology generally), there are different opinions on this. It's typically an even number, because this makes it easier to divide the page. Numbers divisible by three are most used. (If you're interested in knowing why, the Wikipedia article on the golden ratio[1] provides a nice explanation). Popular column values are 12, 16 and 24, but I'll focus on the 12-column grid system here. 12 is popular, as it can be divided into a variety of commonly used sizes, such as a half, a third, and a quarter.

Creating Your Own Grid

You may be wondering how a 12-column layout helps you create a 3-column layout like our example page—and yes, it's confusing at first.

The columns are more used as structural underpinnings, and through CSS you define how many columns you want your elements to span. To make this clearer, here's an example of the 12-column 1180px grid:

[1.] http://en.wikipedia.org/wiki/Golden_ratio

3-7. A 12-column, 1180px grid

And here's how the grid will represent this page (yes, grids within grids, or "nested grids", are okay):

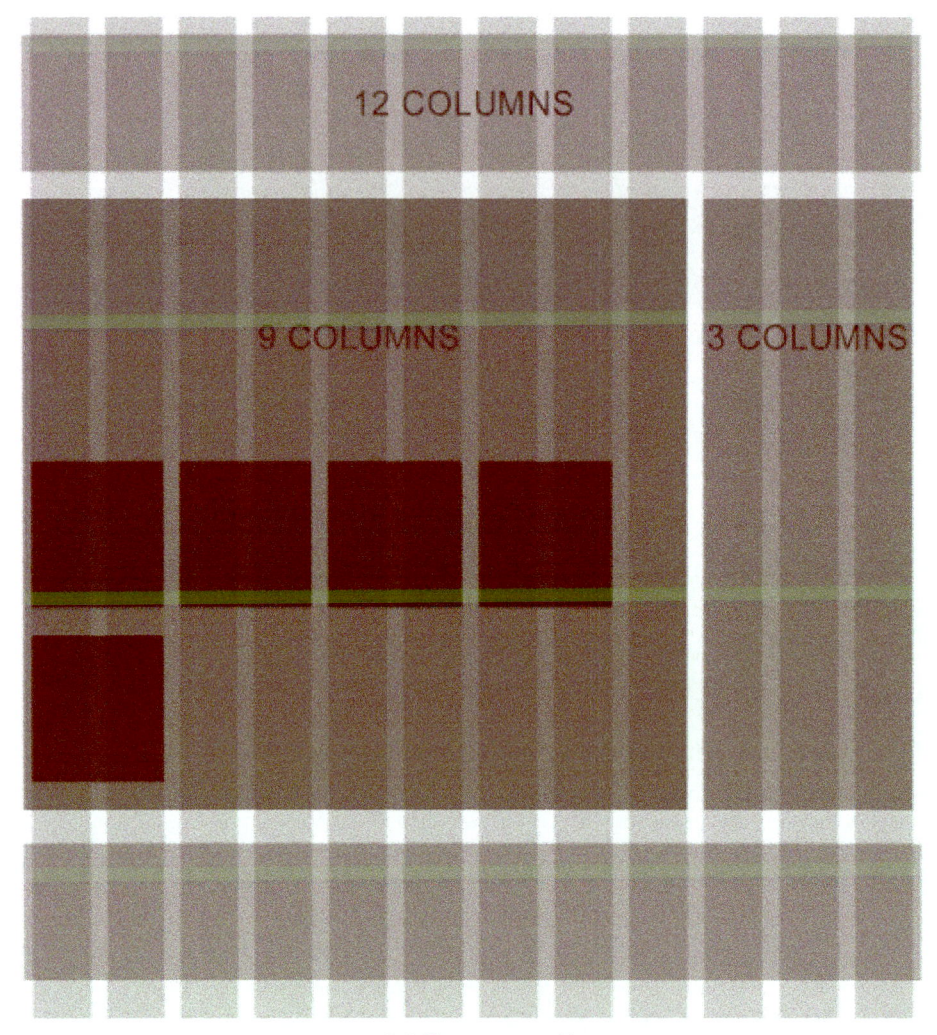

3-8. The page as a grid

You could set up all these columns and grids manually for each project, but it's a much better idea to make something more usable and reusable. We're going to create a lot of new styles and changes to our HTML and CSS files now. Then I'll show easier ways to achieve the same result. Sometimes it's a good idea to learn the hard way before knowing how to make it easier.

Set up the base styles for the columns and rows, and replace any existing matching classes:

3-9. Chapter3/vanilla_final/layout.css *(excerpt)*

```css
.row,
.column {
    box-sizing: border-box;
}

.row:before,
.row:after {
    content: " ";
    display: table;
}

.row:after {
    clear: both;
}

.column {
    position: relative;
    float: left;
}

.column + .column {
    margin-left: 1.6%;
}
```

Using the Adjacent Sibling Selector

The adjacent sibling selector (+) above is a useful CSS trick that adds a margin only to the matching element following another matching element. In our case, it means that the first column won't have a left margin.

The first step is to define the width of one column, not forgetting the margin between each column.

A single column width is equal to 100 (as we're working with percentages) minus the margin value, multiplied by the number of columns minus 1 (you don't need a left margin in the first column), all divided by the number of columns.

If you prefer to look at formulas:

```
SingleColumnWidth = (100 - (MarginValue * (NumberOfColumns -
↪ 1))) / NumberOfColumns
```

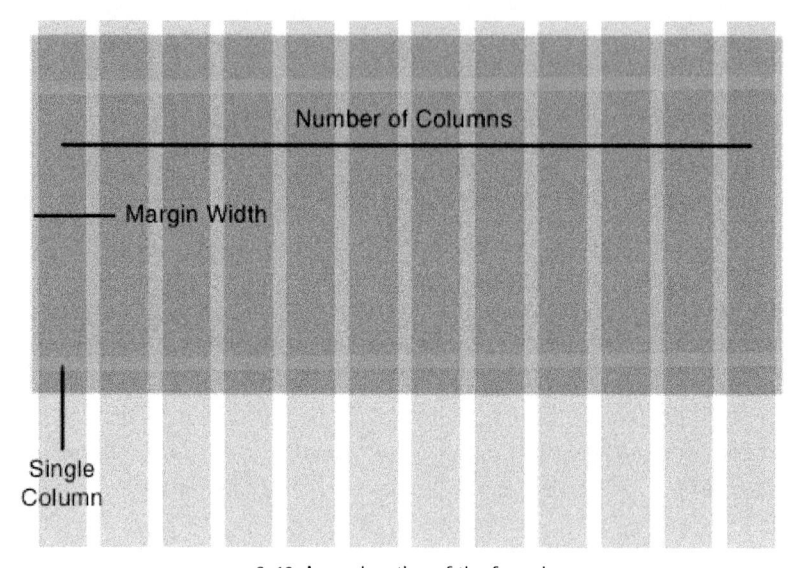

3-10. An explanation of the formula

This should give the nice, memorable result of 6.86666666667% … but don't worry: a number like this is what's expected, and after the initial setup, you won't need to remember these values.

Next, apply this number into a new formula for each of the columns. You want to know the width values of column *spans*—that is, how to spread content across more than one column.

A column width is equal to the `SingleColumnWidth` value multiplied by the current column, added to the margin value multiplied by the number of columns minus 1.

Or as a formula:

```
ColumnWidth = (SingleColumnWidth * CurrentColumn) +
↪ (MarginValue * (CurrentColumn - 1))
```

As an example. here's how to find the value required to span two columns:

```
(SingleColumnWidth * CurrentColumn)
6.86666666667 * 2 = 13.733333333

(CurrentColumn - 1)
2 - 1 = 1

(MarginValue * (CurrentColumn - 1))
1.6 * 1 = 1.6

 (SingleColumnWidth * CurrentColumn) + (MarginValue *
↪ (CurrentColumn - 1))
13.733333333 + 1.6 = 15.333333333
```

This will result in the following column styles, with the `column-n` class representing the number of columns you want to span. Add these to `layout.css`:

3-11. Chapter3/vanilla_final/layout.css *(excerpt)*

```css
.column-1 {
    width: 6.86666666667%;
}

.column-2 {
    width: 15.3333333333%;
}

.column-3 {
    width: 23.8%;
}

.column-4 {
    width: 32.2666666667%;
}

.column-5 {
    width: 40.7333333333%;
}

.column-6 {
    width: 49.2%;
}

.column-7 {
    width: 57.6666666667%;
}

.column-8 {
    width: 66.1333333333%;
}

.column-9 {
    width: 74.6%;
}

.column-10 {
    width: 83.0666666667%;
}
```

```css
.column-11 {
    width: 91.5333333333%;
}

.column-12 {
    width: 100%;
}
```

Again, don't worry about remembering what these values are. Once they're defined, all that's needed is to use the CSS class.

> **Saving Some Legwork**
>
> You could also use a CSS preprocessor—such as Sass or Less—that provides an extra framework to help generate repetitive and complex CSS for you. Among other features, this includes making the calculations above for you.

Now you want the `header` and `nav` bar to always take up 12 columns to better fit into the grid model, so let's rearrange the header and navigation elements into rows and add appropriate column classes. These are the base `column` class and a `column-12` class to fill 12 columns:

```html
<header class="row">
    <h1 class="column column-12">Site Name</h1>
</header>
<nav class="row">
    <ul class="column column-12">
    <li><a href="#">Menu Item</a></li>
    <li><a href="#">Menu Item</a></li>
    <li><a href="#">Menu Item</a></li>
    </ul>
</nav>
```

The left content area needs to be nine columns wide, and the aside three columns, so add those classes:

```html
<section class="showslisting column column-9">
    ...
</section>

<aside class="column column-3">
    ...
</aside>
```

Now add column classes to the TV shows *inside* the content area:

```html
<section class="tvshow column column-2">
    ...
</section>
```

In the `tvshow` class you can now remove the `width` and `display` properties and change the height to `auto` for more responsive magic:

```css
section.tvshow {
    height: auto;
}
```

The page layout doesn't look too much different from how it did before, but these crucial changes allow for increased flexibility. Want to make the TV show listings tighter? Then change the class to `column-3`.

Want a wider aside menu? Change its class to `column-4` and change the listings width class to `column-8`:

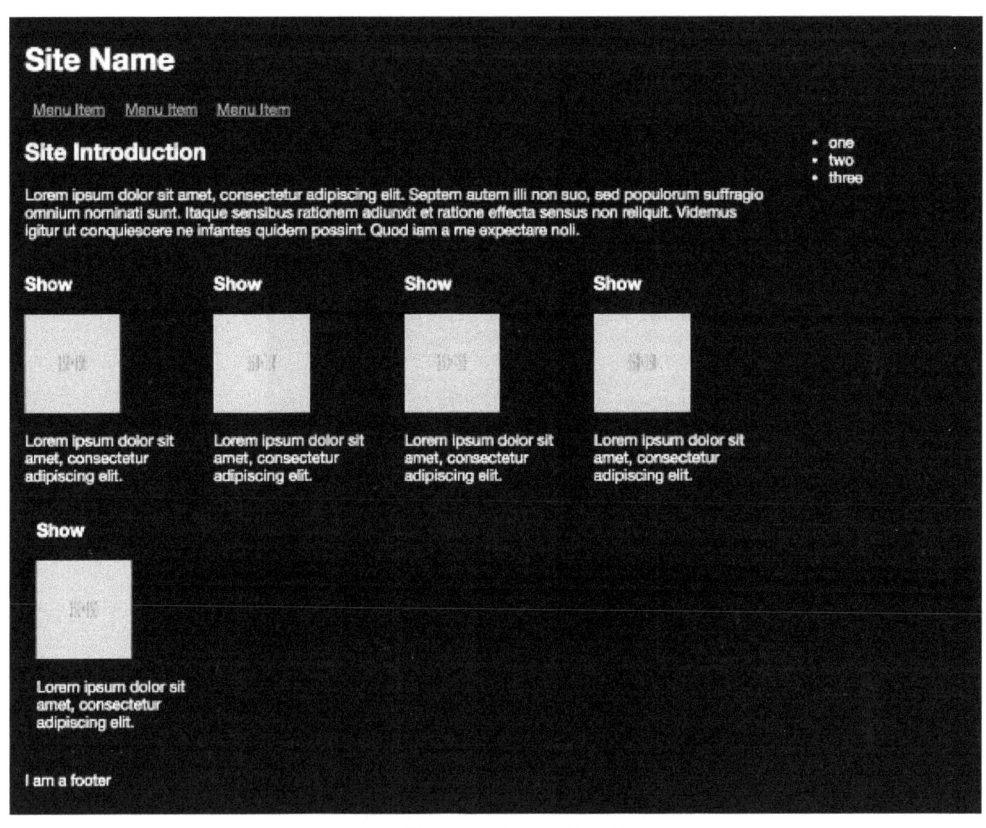

3-12. The page with a wider aside

As the browser window changes size, you'll see page elements shrink and grow smoothly, perfect for responsive web design. But notice what happens when you get to a smaller screen size:

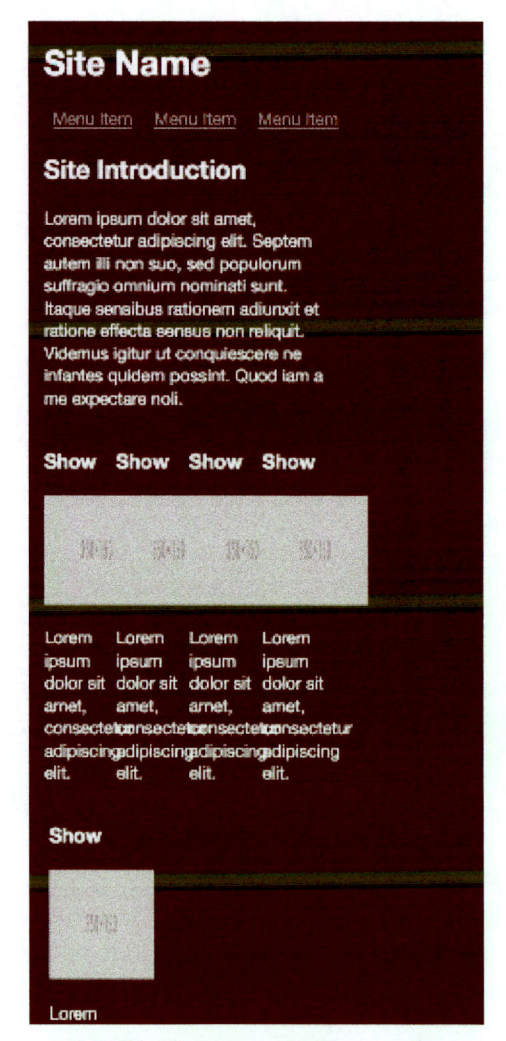

3-13. What happens on a smaller screen size

Not a great look: the TV show elements have become squashed. Some of this is due to the images not having reduced appropriately in size yet—a topic we'll cover further in Chapter 5. This is also a problem with a fluid grid. In theory, what should happen at smaller screen sizes is that the main content column should instead fill 100% of the screen's width, or the class should change to `column-12` to fill the full width of the screen.

One solution is to override the percentage width of the `column-8` class at relevant breakpoints. For example:

```
section.showslisting.column-8 {
    width: 100%;
}
...
@media only screen and (min-width: 992px) {
    ...
    section.showslisting.column-8 {
        width: 66%;
    }
    ...
}
```

But this is a poor solution, and you'll soon lose track of what class equals what size.

You could change the class applied to the div with JavaScript, and in the past, this was a solution to the problem. But instead, I'll show you some more modern (and better) options that will make the principle of grids more useful for responsive design.

Flexbox

While the "column method" above isn't that hard to understand and implement, as your layouts become more complex you can start to introduce a lot of nested `divs` and CSS styles to support them. The example above used `float` to position page elements into the desired position. As the example was simple, it wasn't too hard to achieve this, but as grids get more complex, especially nested grids, `float`s quickly become messy, and the solutions to cope with this aren't ideal.

The CSS Flexible Box ("flexbox") Layout Module is a recent part of the CSS spec and already enjoys good browser support. It was designed to provide a better and more modern solution for this type of layout, offering you specific functionality for the task.

After an initial page restructure and learning new concepts, you'll find that using flexbox for your page components will drastically simplify your HTML structure and CSS classes.

Everything that you want flexbox to manage is contained within a "flex container". Much like earlier examples, begin with the code from the start of this chapter and continue to use a containing `div`:

```
<div class="container">
    ...
</div>
```

And the CSS for this container:

3-14. Chapter3/flexbox/layout.css *(excerpt)*

```
.container {
    display: flex;
    flex-flow: row wrap;
}
```

The `display` property is set to `flex` to enable flexbox layout. The `flex-flow` property is shorthand for two other properties.

The first of these properties is `flex-direction`, which defines how the individual items inside a flex container will be placed. The two most common values are `row` and `column`. Using `row` will place items horizontally (left to right or right to left, depending on your preference). And `column` works similarly, but instead places elements from top to bottom. You can reverse the direction by appending with `-reverse`.

The `flex` display mode is one-dimensional (running either horizontally or vertically) and will attempt to keep fitting items on one line. The `flex-wrap` property determines what will happen if the container can't fit all items on one line. The items can be set to `wrap` to the next line or be forced into one line with `nowrap`.

Next, let's handle the `header`, `nav`, and `footer` page elements, which fill the entire width of the page container. Replace any existing styles with the following:

3-15. Chapter3/flexbox/layout.css *(excerpt)*

```
header, nav, footer {
    flex: 1 100%;
}
```

`flex` is shorthand for three combined properties, in the following order:

- `flex-grow` determines how much space an item is allowed to use in a container, and the sizes are relative to each other. If every item in a container has a `flex-grow` value of 1, then each item is evenly distributed. If one item has a value of 2, it will take up twice as much space as the other items.
- `flex-shrink` determines whether or not an item can shrink to less than its `flex-grow` value, and if so, to which value. The default is 1, so if you want to keep proportions no matter what, leave the value empty.
- `flex-basis` allows you to set a default item size before space is distributed, in any of the typical CSS sizing units.

Moving to the main content area, again replacing any existing styles, you can also remove any of the previous methods for resizing elements inside media queries:

3-16. Chapter3/flexbox/layout.css *(excerpt)*

```css
main {
    flex-grow: 2;
    flex-basis: 66%;
}

aside {
    flex-grow: 1;
    flex-basis: 33%;
}
...
@media only screen and (min-width: 320px) {
    aside {
        display: none;
    }

    section.showslisting {
    }

    .showdescription {
        display: none;
    }
}
…
@media only screen and (min-width: 992px) {
    aside {
        display: block;
    }

    section.showslisting {
    }

    .showdescription {
        white-space: normal;
        width: 125px;
    }
}
```

Resize the page. Notice that you now have the same effect as with the first fluid grid example, but have removed a lot of CSS from the media queries. With one set of flex properties, the sizing of page elements is handled for us. All without the need for any JavaScript!

If you were to restructure the page, you could remove the `flex-basis` properties, but nesting flex containers with different row/column directions would involve further `div` elements, so weigh up your HTML complexity versus CSS complexity.

Next, here are the styles for the TV show listing:

3-17. Chapter3/flexbox/layout.css em>(excerpt)

```css
section.showslisting {
    display: flex;
    flex-wrap: wrap;
    flex-direction: row;
    margin-bottom: 25px;
}

section.tvshow {
    width: 125px;
    height: auto;
}
```

This sets the `showlistings` section as another flex container that wraps any items that don't fit onto one line—since, by default, flex will try to fit all items onto one line.

At this point, you can also delete the `left` class from your HTML and CSS, as it's no longer needed.

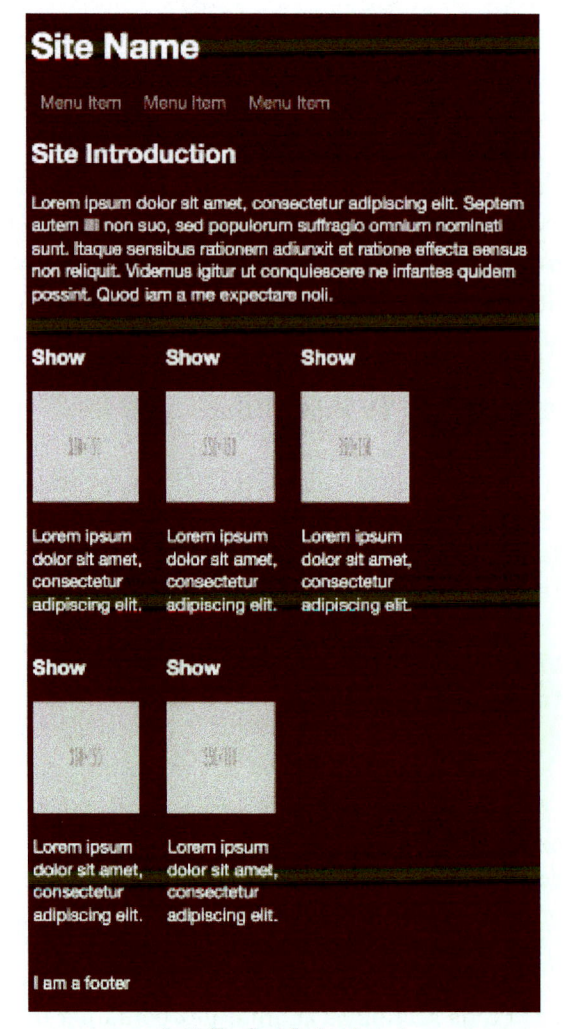

3-18. The final flexbox layout

One other cool flexbox trick is to set the order of elements using the `order` property, and a number that defines its position. For example, you could use the following to rearrange page elements on a mobile device:

```
nav { order: 1;}
header { order: 2;}
main { order: 3;}
footer { order: 4;}
```

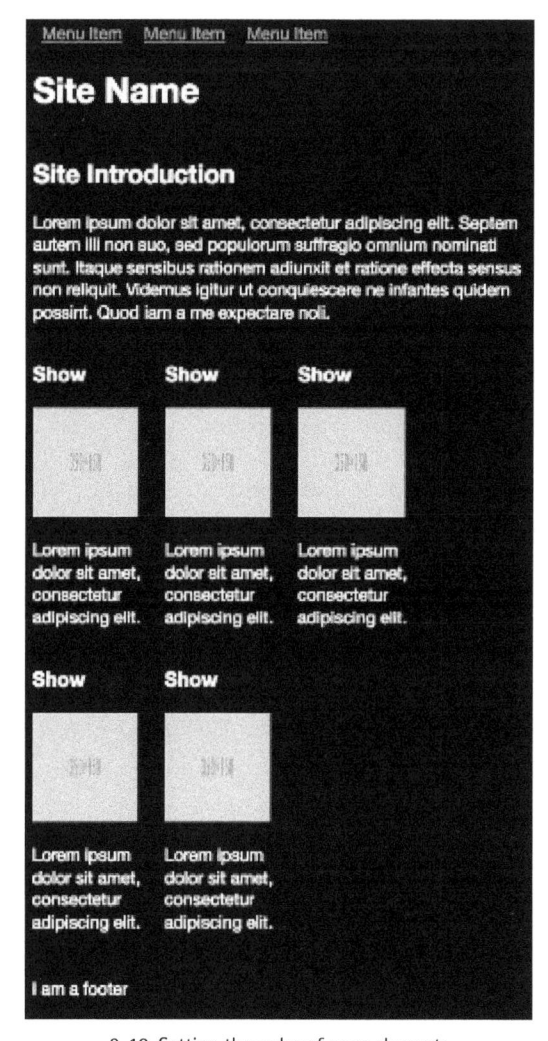

3-19. Setting the order of page elements

But if you wanted to remove page elements, you'd still need to use media queries.

This has been a brief example of how to use flexbox, but as you can see, once you've restructured your page, flexbox handles a lot of the manual page reflowing work for you.

CSS Grid Layout

Complementary to flexbox is the CSS Grid Layout Module, which helps you define and lay out the regions of a page. In the past, the main option open to web developers for flexible (I use this term loosely) page layouts was using HTML tables to define page areas with rows and columns, but these were terrible for accessibility. The grid layout is something of a modern re-interpretation of that concept.

> **Browser Support for Grid Layout**
>
> Grid shipped for all the newest versions of the major browsers in early 2017, so a fallback strategy is required if your layouts need to be supported in older browsers. You can check online[2] for details on which browser versions do and don't support Grid.

Let's try applying the grid layout to the demo site, starting with the code from the beginning of this chapter,[3].

Again, make a container `div` inside the `body` to contain the layout:

```
...
<div class="container">
...
</div>
...
```

Move the `aside` from inside `main` to outside of it. This lets you treat it like a proper column in its own right:

---

[2] https://caniuse.com/#feat=css-grid
[3] https://github.com/spbooks/responsive2/blob/master/code/Chapter3/chapter_start/index.html

> 3-20. Chapter3/grid/index.html *(excerpt)*

```html
...
</main>
<aside class="left">
    <ul>
    <li>one</li>
    <li>two</li>
    <li>three</li>
    </ul>
</aside>
```

In the CSS, change the `display` type to `grid`:

```css
.container {
    display: grid;
}
```

Now the grid display gets really cool. Add the following:

> 3-21. Chapter3/grid/layout.css *(excerpt)*

```css
.container {
    display: grid;
    grid-template-columns: 66% 33%;
}
```

> **Removing Sizing Overrides**
>
> As with the flexbox layout, you can also take this opportunity to remove all the other sizing overrides in media queries.

And in one simple CSS property, you've removed the need for two of the CSS classes used so far. The `grid-template-columns` property gives you even more possibilities. For example:

- You can use any standard sizing unit for defining the column, including `auto` to fill remaining space.
- You can use `fr` ("fractional units") to let the grid proportionately fill space. So you could rewrite this grid as `grid-template-columns: 2fr 1fr;`, which means that the first column will fill two-thirds of the space, and the second one third.

Great, but if you look at the demo site now, you'll notice that the rows in the design that don't have a 66/33 split don't look right. This is because you also need to define the rows with similar syntax:

3-22. Chapter3/grid/layout.css *(excerpt)*

```css
.container {
    display: grid;
    grid-template-columns: 66% 33%;
    grid-template-rows: 80px 80px auto 20px;
}
```

How Many Rows?

This is the first example where we've needed to explicitly define rows, and there are a couple of ways you could do it. I suggest that there are four rows: the title, the top menu, the introductory text and TV shows, and the footer. If you want to change these divisions (for example, splitting the description and TV shows), feel free to do so.

This syntax specifies a set height for three elements and then lets the remaining TV shows element fill the remaining empty space.

But again, if you load the page in the browser, little has changed. In fact, the `footer` has now jumped up the page. This is because there's one more step needed—to add the sub-elements into the grid:

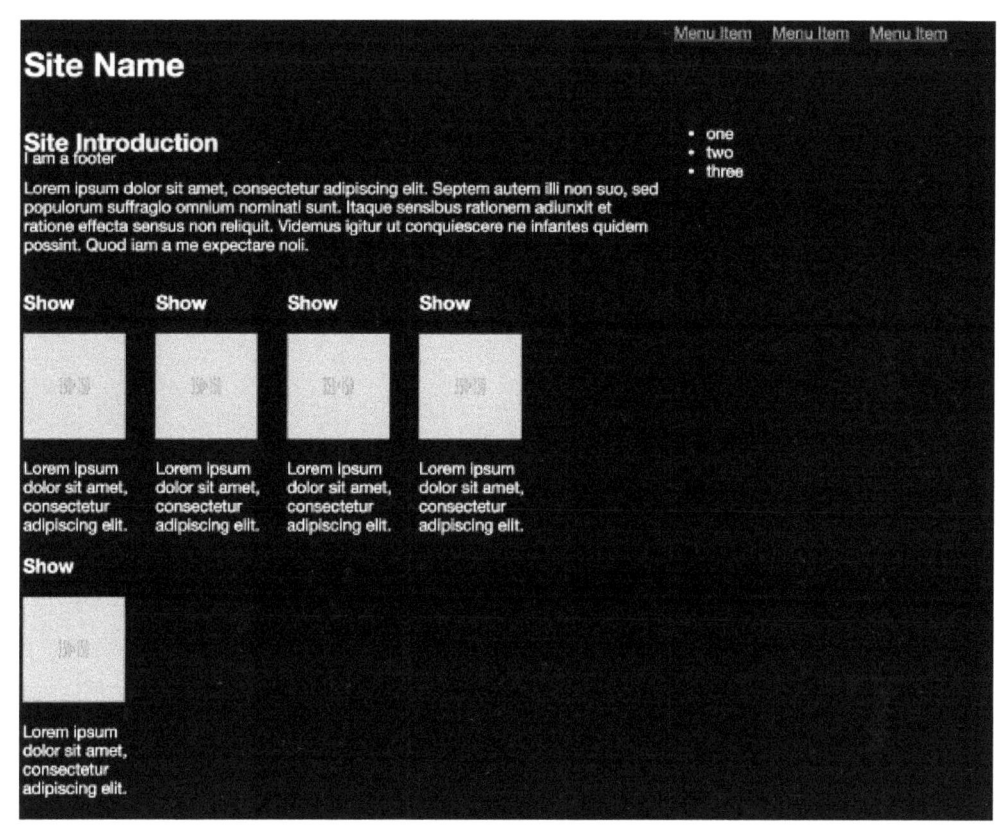

3-23. Sub-elements not yet added

The grid display layout has two interesting methods for defining where you can place an item.

1. The first is similar to flexbox, allowing you to specify an order number.
2. The second lets you place items at named locations. To use this method, you need to define what are called **line names**.

The code below sets the `display` style to `grid`, then defines the columns and rows you need. For the columns, this is a column named `left` that's 66% of the page width, and a column named `right` that fills 33%. For the rows this defines three with a fixed height (`header`, `main-nav` and `footer`) and `shows` will automatically fill any remaining space.

```
.container {
    display: grid;
```

```
    grid-template-columns: [left] 66% [right] 33%;
    grid-template-rows: [header] 80px [main-nav] 40px [shows]
    auto [footer] 20px;
}
```

At this point, now you understand what's going on, it's time to make this mobile first. Change the current `container` class to the following:

```
.container {
    display: grid;
    grid-template-columns: [left] 100%;
    grid-template-rows: [header] 80px [main-nav] 40px [shows]
    auto [footer] 20px;
}
```

And for larger screen sizes:

```
@media only screen and (min-width: 992px) {
    .container {
    grid-template-columns: [left] 66% [right] 33%;
    }
    …
}
```

If you've ever created tables in a desktop publishing application (or remember using tables for layout in the dark days of web design), you'll know that you need to define how an item "spans" across multiple cells or rows. The technique is the same with the grid display. Take the `header` as an example:

```
header {
    grid-column-start: left;
    grid-column-end: right;
    grid-row-start: header;
    grid-row-end: header;
```

```
}
```

This declaration block states that the column should start at the left and span all the way to the right, as well as span from the top to the bottom of that row.

The other page elements follow a similar pattern:

```
...
nav {
    grid-column-start: left;
    grid-column-end: right;
    grid-row-start: main-nav;
    grid-row-end: main-nav;
}
...
main {
    grid-column-start: left;
    grid-column-end: right;
    grid-row-start: shows;
    grid-row-end: shows;
}
...
footer {
    grid-column-start: left;
    grid-column-end: right;
    grid-row-start: footer;
    grid-row-end: footer;
}
...
@media only screen and (min-width: 992px) {
    ...
    aside {
    display: block;
    grid-column-start: right;
    grid-column-end: right;
    grid-row-start: header;
    grid-row-end: header;
    }
```

```
}
```

And now you have a grid defined. Initially, the syntax seems verbose, but it's more human readable.

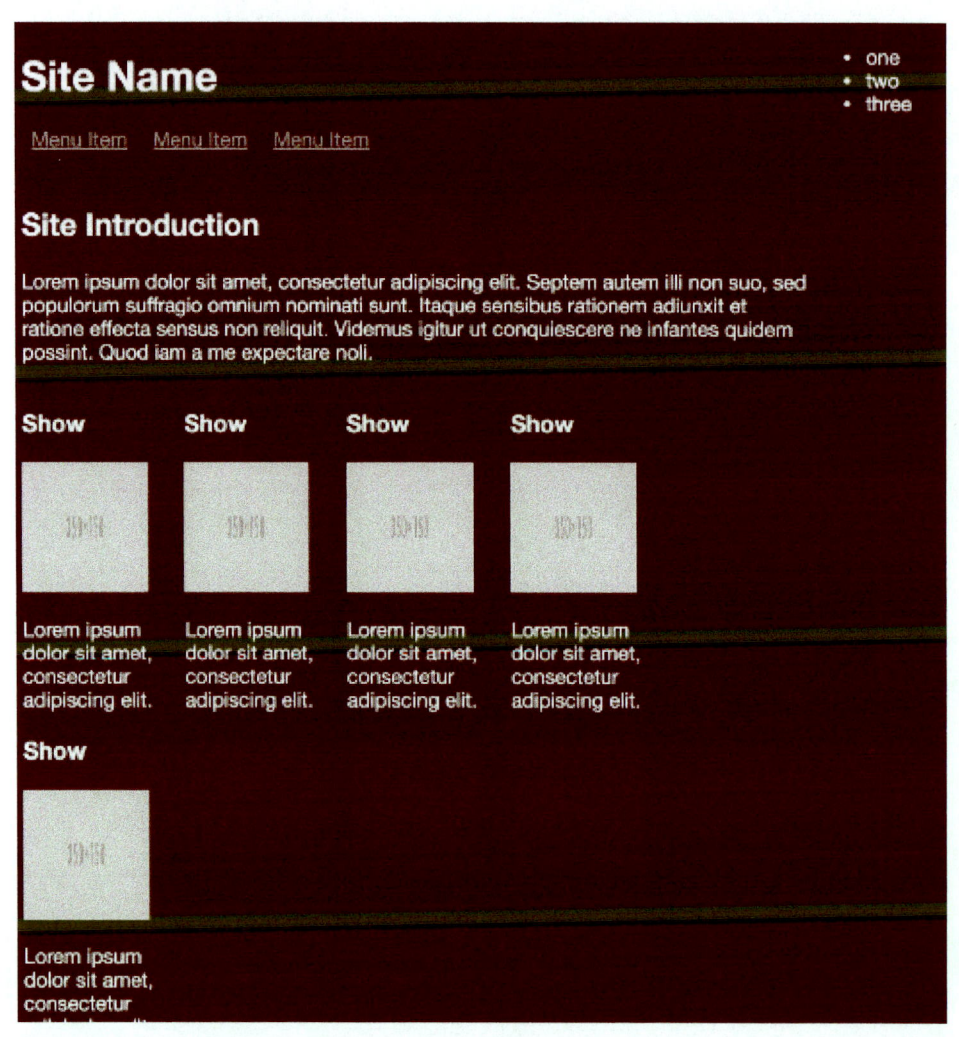

3-24. The final grid layout

There are lots of other grid layout features, including repeating layouts, nested grids, content alignment, and the ability to define margins and spacing in your grids. One final advantage of the grid display is that it also makes floating and clearing unnecessary, so remove the `left` class from the HTML and any clearing styles that were used.

Making Grids Easier with Frameworks

In many cases, creating a grid in the way described in this chapter isn't too much work, but developers and designers like to reduce repetitive tasks as much as possible. A simple solution is to create your own grid system that works for you and reuse it across your projects. But of course, other developers and designers have thought the same thing and have provided their grid systems (or frameworks) on the internet. I'll present two of the popular ones, but it's a topic where opinions are many and change is rapid. My aim here is to show you how frameworks *may* be able to help you save time on repetitive tasks, rather than go into detail over which one is "better" (a decision you'll have to make for yourself). Many of these frameworks supply more than responsive grids, providing other responsive elements such as fonts, icons, and reusable widgets. You may prefer one framework over another because it gives you better options for other aspects of your web pages.

Bootstrap

While not the first framework for responsive design, Bootstrap[4] is the most widely used. You've probably seen it in action without realizing. Released in 2011 by Twitter, it uses a 12-column grid, offers flexbox layout, and has periodically had one of the most popular repositories on GitHub.

Popularity is Bootstrap's biggest advantage and disadvantage. It's easy to use, encourages positive layout and CSS practices, and has plenty of documentation and community help. But your site can easily end up looking a lot like every other Bootstrap-powered site.

Installing Bootstrap

The default download of Bootstrap can add a lot to the weight of your page, so I recommend you take a good look at the instructions[5] to ensure you get a copy

---

[4]. http://getbootstrap.com/

that's best optimized for your use. For this example, I'll use the CDN option, as it's the simplest. If you want to follow along, add the lines provided on the Bootstrap page, and remove the link to the current CSS file.

You can find the simplified (no media queries) refactored `index.html` page in the code archive[6] as an example. You've lost the custom font and background colors, which would be easy to re-add, but you have a responsive grid (Bootstrap also uses a 12-column grid) without too much effort, and that works in a similar way to our custom grid. Bootstrap also has a lot of other styles available for handling images, determining what grid elements to display at different grid sizes, and much, much more.

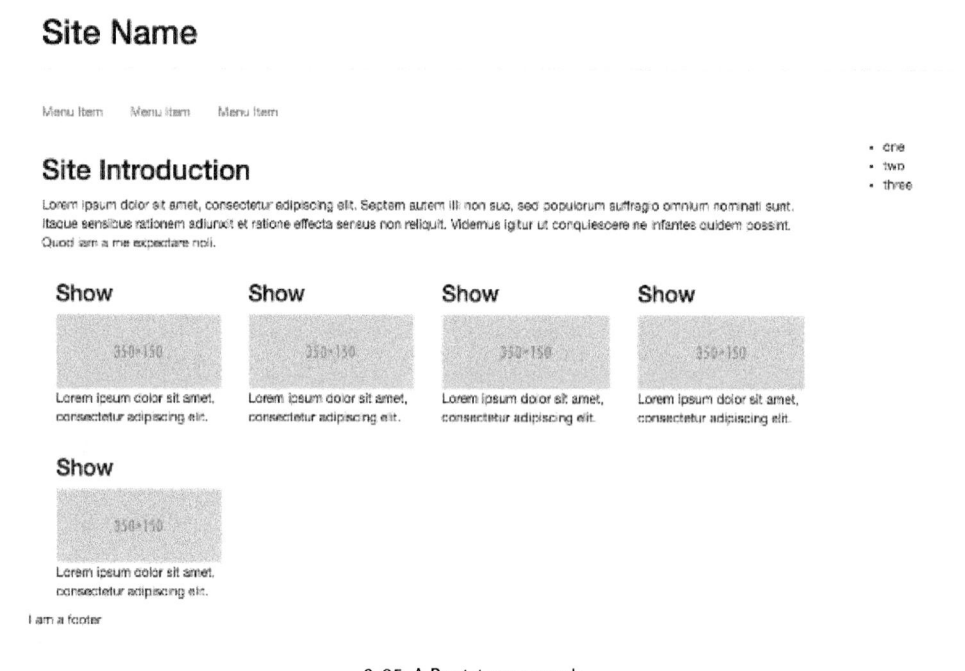

3-25. A Bootstrap example

If you're interested in learning more about Bootstrap, I recommend SitePoint's *Jump Start Bootstrap*[7].

[5.] http://getbootstrap.com/getting-started/#download

[6.] https://github.com/spbooks/responsive2/blob/master/code/Chapter3/bootstrap/index.html

[7.] https://www.sitepoint.com/premium/books/jump-start-bootstrap

Foundation

Foundation[8] was created in 2011 by Zurb (an interactive design agency). It also offers a lot of features (including optional flexbox), has regular releases, and a good community, but is less widely used. It provides more flexibility to create layouts (based on a 12-column grid), but generally requires more classes and layout elements to achieve this.

Installing Foundation

Like Bootstrap, Foundation can add a lot of page weight, so make sure you download the best configuration for you[9].

Remove the current stylesheet and add links to the new stylesheets:

```
<link rel="stylesheet"
 href="foundation/css/foundation.css">
<link rel="stylesheet" href="foundation/css/app.css">
```

You can find the Foundation simplified (no media queries) refactored `index.html` file in the code archive[10] as an example. Again, you've lost the custom colors that can be replaced, but you should be able to see the extra elements and classes you need to add.

---

[8] http://foundation.zurb.com/
[9] http://foundation.zurb.com/sites/download.html/
[10] https://github.com/spbooks/responsive2/blob/master/code/Chapter3/foundation/index.html

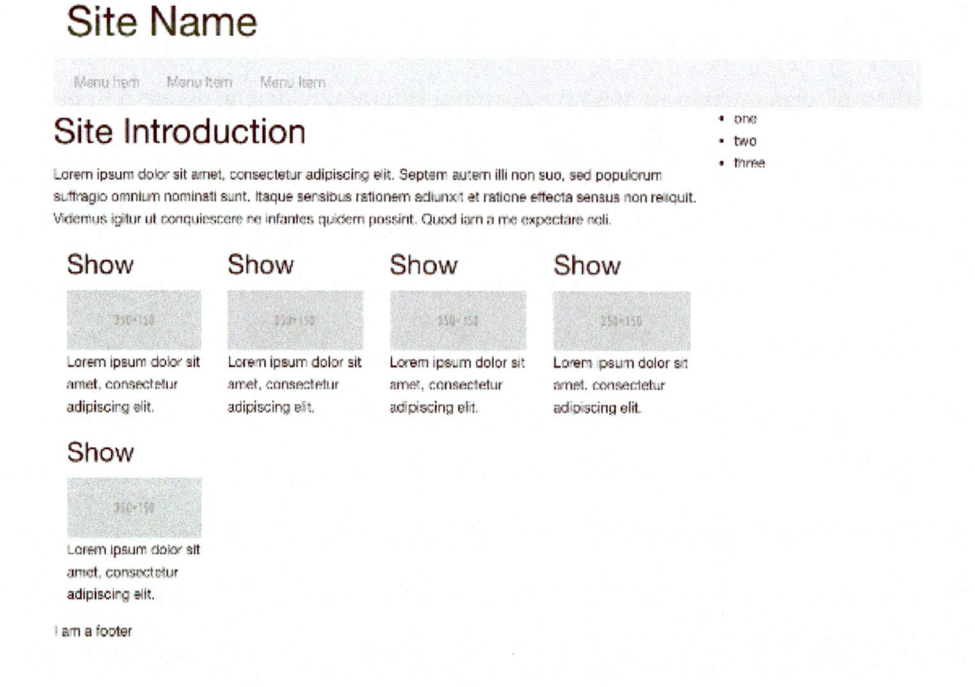

3-26. A Foundation example

If you're interested in learning more about Foundation, then I recommend SitePoint's *Jump Start Foundation*[11].

What About the Demo App?

I've used sections of the demo app so far in examples for this chapter, but the rest of the book will not use any grid systems. This is for clarity, so you can more easily see the examples covering other topics without the grids getting in the way, but also to reduce compatibility issues with certain browsers.

As an exercise, try picking your favorite grid system from this chapter and rewriting future examples using it.

[11.] https://www.sitepoint.com/premium/books/jump-start-foundation

Wrap Up

Now you know how to make a page layout that can respond to any browser size and always fit proportionally. In the next chapter, we'll look at making the content inside the layout responsive—because, without readable and presentable content on all devices, your work is not yet complete.

Chapter 4

Responsive Text

If web pages are to be truly responsive, then the content of pages should also flow and change to suit the dimensions of the device a user is viewing it on. While web pages are becoming more image and media heavy, text is still a crucial component, and there are numerous techniques to help make it as readable as possible, no matter the current device.

To understand better the ways you can represent text on a web page, it's best to take a trip into the long history of text.

The History of Text

The principles of **typography** (the arranging and styling of text) have been evolving for as long as people have been printing words on pages. Measurements such as leading (the space between lines of text), kerning (the space between letters) and tracking (the space between words) have carried over to desktop publishing, and anyone who's used QuarkXpress, InDesign, or their predecessors, will know how they affect text.

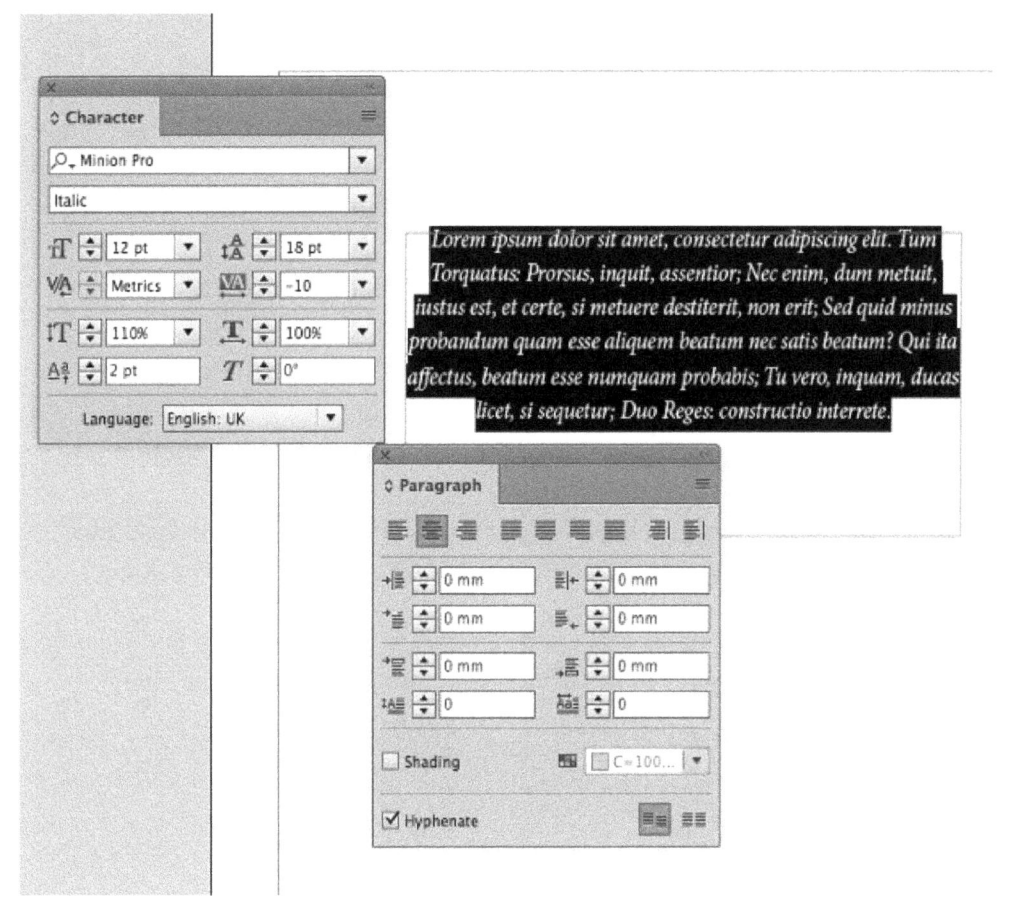

4-1. Text formatting in Adobe InDesign

Manual typesetting was a laborious process, as it involved tweaking the leading, kerning and tracking of every line of text. Desktop publishing, and more recently setting type with CSS, has made it far easier to play with these properties in an attempt to get the "perfect" text.

CSS typography shares many of the same properties as print typography but has some different names. In fact, it has more descriptive names than the older print version.

In the early days of the Web, the level of typographic control was limited, but CSS3 has helped greatly, giving us more tools to realize our designs.

Responsive Typographical Properties in CSS

There are lots of text-related properties you can set with CSS. Here are some that I consider the most useful for responsive design:

- `font-size`: the size of the font.
- `line-height`: specifies the minimum height of lines within `block` elements, and the actual line height of inline elements.
- `font-weight`: the "weight" of the font, or how bold and strong it is.
- `text-decoration`: used to set either underline or strike-through.
- `text-align`: used to set text alignment of left, right, center, or justified (aligned to the left and right margins equally).
- `text-transform`: used to make text display as uppercase, lowercase or capitalized.
- `letter-spacing`: specifies the spacing between letters, much like leading.
- `word-spacing`: specifies the spacing between words, much like tracking.

It's common to set some or all of these properties with pixel values. For example, you could add the following to the `body` selector of the current demo site:

```
body {
    font-size: 18px;
    line-height: 22px;
    letter-spacing: 4px;
}
```

This will result in text that looks like this:

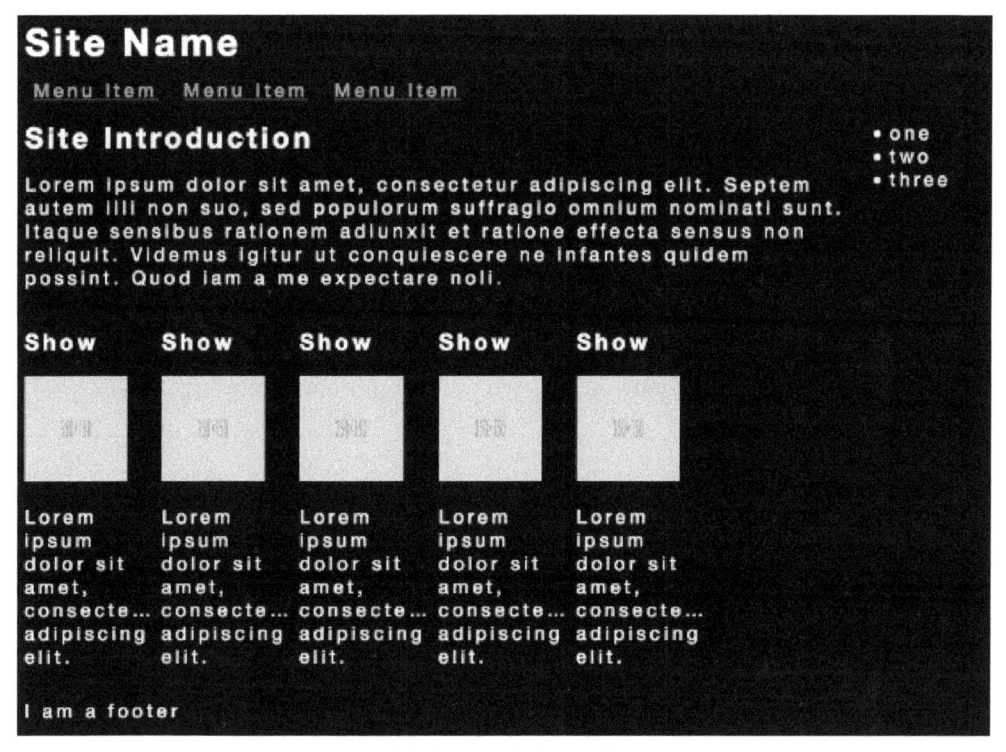

4-2. A strange text example

Other properties you may find useful in your designs are:

- `font-style`: sets text to italic or oblique. Italic text may not be as readable on small screen as on large screens.
- `text-indent`: sets the indentation (mostly) of the first line of text in a block of text. With space at a premium on smaller devices, it may be better to indent paragraphs than to set spaces between them.
- `text-align-last`: sets the alignment of the last line of a text block. Again, at different devices sizes, you may want to handle this differently.
- `white-space`: defines the handling of white space and wrapping in a block of text.
- `word-wrap`: specifies if words are allowed to break over lines. This could be useful for optimizing text based on display size.

You may be wondering how setting text at fixed sizes could be responsive. 18px is 18px whether it's rendered on a desktop computer or a mobile screen. You could use media queries to set different font sizes at various screen sizes, but this would become arduous, and there's potentially a better method.

CSS allows you to use different units for sizing elements, but especially with text. They fall into two camps: fixed sizing and relative sizing.

Fixed Sizing

Fixed sizing means that the size is always the same. There are seven possible units you can use, but I'll focus on the two most common, `px` and `pt` values.

Pixels

Pixels are those little dots of color that comprise the screens of every device. When you need to set the size of an element in HTML, one CSS pixel equals one device pixel, right? Well, no...

Device pixels (also called **screen pixels**) are the actual pixels comprising your screen, and traditionally this was the number of pixels in the width by height of a user's screen. This may not be the same as the size of their browser window, as desktop users frequently resize it, and browsers don't typically operate in full-screen mode.

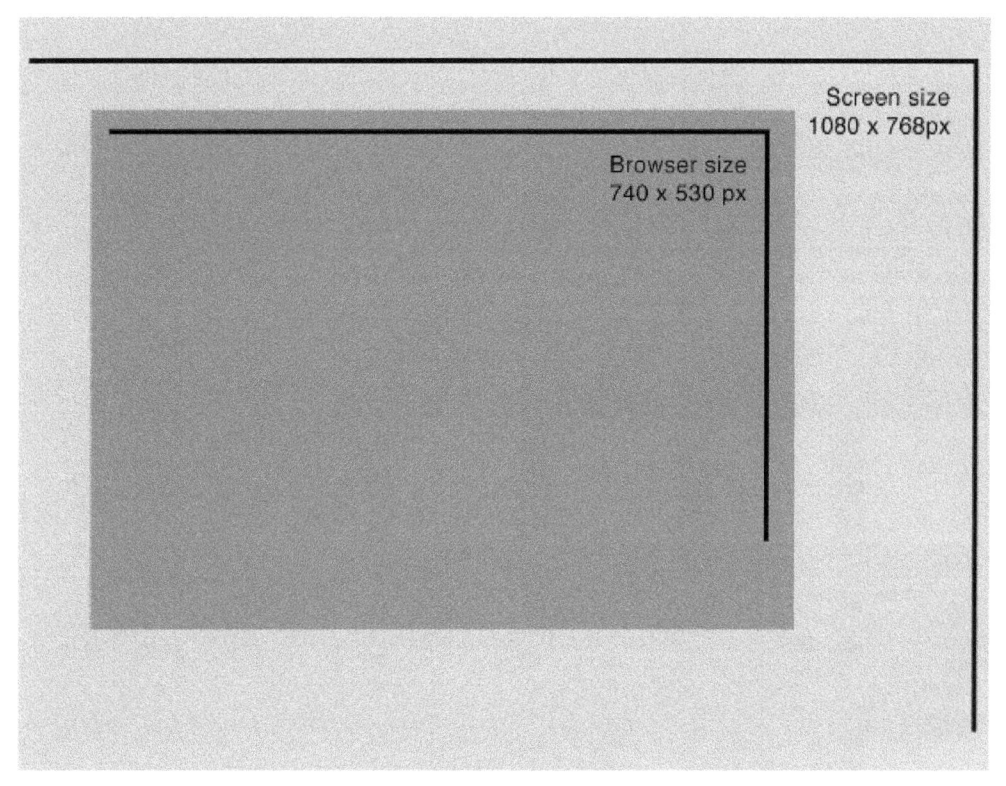

4-3. Screen size vs browser size

The newer, high-resolution screens—such as Apple's "Retina" displays—complicate matters, as they use a larger number of pixels over the same screen area. Typically, this is achieved by doubling the number of pixels vertically and horizontally—though increasing numbers of screens have four times as many pixels in each direction.

Complicating this further are users who scale or zoom their browser windows for accessibility or other reasons. For example, the screenshot below is the current demo site zoomed to 125%, where one *CSS pixel* now covers 1.25 *device pixels*.

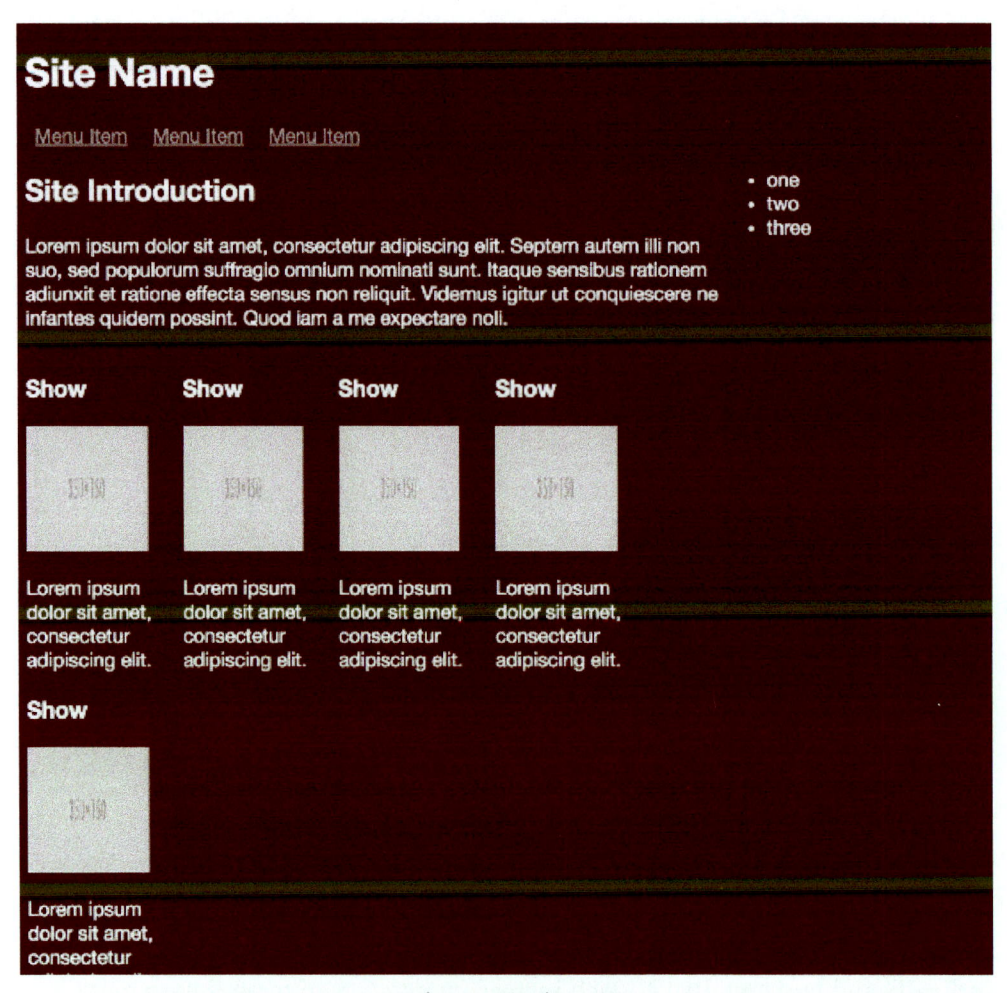

4-4. A page zoomed to 125%

For these reasons, it's best to ignore actual device pixels and focus on **CSS pixels**—the pixel values you set in your CSS file. The CSS pixel value is a more accurate number, which takes into account the factors outlined above. Browsers also handle a lot of the scaling issues for you.

The **pixel** (px) sizing unit theoretically represents the size of one pixel of a screen. In relation to text, this means that when setting text to 16px, the length of the lowest point in the text (such as the bottom of a lowercase 'g') to the highest point (such as the top of a lowercase 'h') is 16px.

4-5. Text height includes ascenders and descenders

For other properties, such as `letter-spacing`, this literally means the number of pixels between characters at their widest point.

Points

As you saw in the earlier screenshot from InDesign, the **point** (`pt`) sizing unit has its heritage in print text and is more confusing to understand. It represents a similar size to the pixels example, but as different operating systems and screens represent pixels to points in different ways, they are best reserved for print styles.

Relative Sizing

Relative sizing is more suited to web and responsive design, as sizes will change relative to a base size. But it's useful to understand fixed sizing (at least pixels) to appreciate how these sizing methods work. The most popular units for relative font sizing are the `%`, `em`, and `rem` values.

The first important fact to know when using relative sizes is what these sizes are relative to. By default in all browsers, it's 16px, but if a user has changed this default—for example, to compensate for low vision—then relative sizes will still scale up and down proportionally.

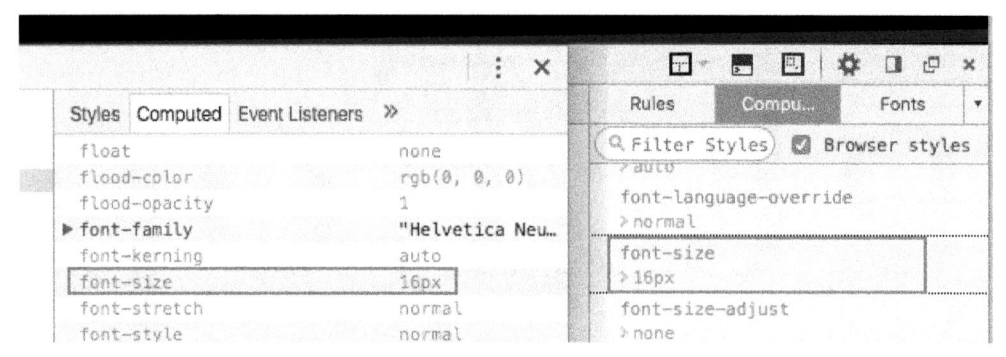

4-6. Default font sizes

Percent

Setting a percentage value for a font size means making it a percentage of the default font size, so if a user has the font size of their browser set at 16px, then `font-size: 100%;` will still equal 16px, and `font-size: 50%` will equal 8px.

As an example, let's try applying percentage sizing to the demo site, again with a mobile first approach, setting the base font size for users of devices with smaller screens.

> **We're Assuming a Base Font Size of 16px**
>
> For these examples, I'll assume that the base font size is the default **16px**. If it's different in your browser, then the sizes stated will be different.

Add a base font size to the **body** element that sets the default font size to 75% of 16px, which is 12px:

```
body {
    font-size: 75%;
}
```

Then, in the tablet and desktop media queries, add font sizes for the larger screen sizes:

```
...
@media only screen and (min-width: 768px) {
    body {
        font-size: 100%;
    }
}

@media only screen and (min-width: 992px) {
    body {
        font-size: 125%;
    }
}
```

This results in a subtly more pixelated font rendering on larger screens than on medium-sized screens.

Em

Despite its recent rise in popularity with web designers, the em unit is an old typographical unit named after the letter "M". The base value of an em unit is equal to the current typeface size in points. For example, one em in a 16-point typeface is 16 points.

In practice, it works in a similar way to percentage sizing, but the units are smaller. So, for example, assuming a default font size of 16px, `font-size: 1em` will still equal 16px, and `font-size: 0.5em` will equal 8px.

The unit values are smaller with `ems`, but it's easy for styles to result in large font sizes accidentally. For example, consider `font-size: 4em`: while the number doesn't look large, it actually equals 64px. Of course, you could set your default font size to something smaller, and then increasing `ems` won't result in such large variations.

As an example, let's try applying em sizing to the demo site, again with a mobile first approach.

Add a base font size to the body element that sets the default font size to .75em of 16px, which is 12px:

```
body {
    font-size: 0.75em;
}
```

Then, in the tablet and desktop media queries, add font sizes for the larger screen sizes:

```
@media only screen and (min-width: 768px) {
    body {
        font-size: 1em;
    }
}

@media only screen and (min-width: 992px) {
    body {
        font-size: 1.25em;
    }
}
```

I won't add screenshots, as the results should look exactly the same as with the percentage examples.

One neat trick with ems is that the relative sizing cascades down nested elements. For example, modify the page's `aside` element to have some nested list items:

```
<aside class="left">
    <ul>
    <li>one
        <ul>
        <li>sub item</li>
        <li>sub item</li>
        </ul>
```

```
        </li>
        <li>two
            <ul>
            <li>sub item</li>
            <li>sub item</li>
            </ul>
        </li>
        <li>three
            <ul>
            <li>sub item</li>
            <li>sub item</li>
            </ul>
        </li>
        </ul>
</aside>
```

Then add the following style:

```
aside ul {
    font-size: 0.75em;
}
```

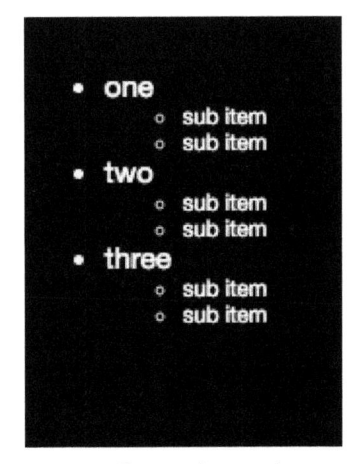

4-7. Em cascade example

You'll see that the font size for the outer `ul` is .75em (15px) of the current default size (in the screenshot this is 20px), and the inner `ul` is .75em of that size (11.25px). While this technique allows for a fantastic shorthand way of creating responsive text sizes that can cascade through your page structure, it requires careful planning, as an element several levels deep may end up smaller or larger than you expect.

Rem

The `rem` unit stands for "root em", and the sizing representation of the unit is the same. But "root" implies that the relative sizing is calculated from one base element—which is the `html` element—rather than the immediate containing element. This gives you a more predictable alternative to ems, as it's easier to tell what the size is relative to.

As an example, let's try applying `rem` sizing to the demo site.

Add a base font size to the `html` of `12px` (assuming a default of 16px):

```css
html {
    font-size: 75%;
}
```

Then inside the tablet and desktop media queries, add font sizes for the larger screen sizes:

```css
@media only screen and (min-width: 768px) {
    html {
        font-size: 1rem;
    }
}

@media only screen and (min-width: 992px) {
    html {
        font-size: 1.25rem;
    }
```

```
}
```

Not much changes when applied to the demo site, as it's effectively the same sizing. Now add the following styles to the nested list example from above:

```
aside ul {
    font-size: 0.75rem;
}
```

Now the sizing is 3/4 of the current base font size.

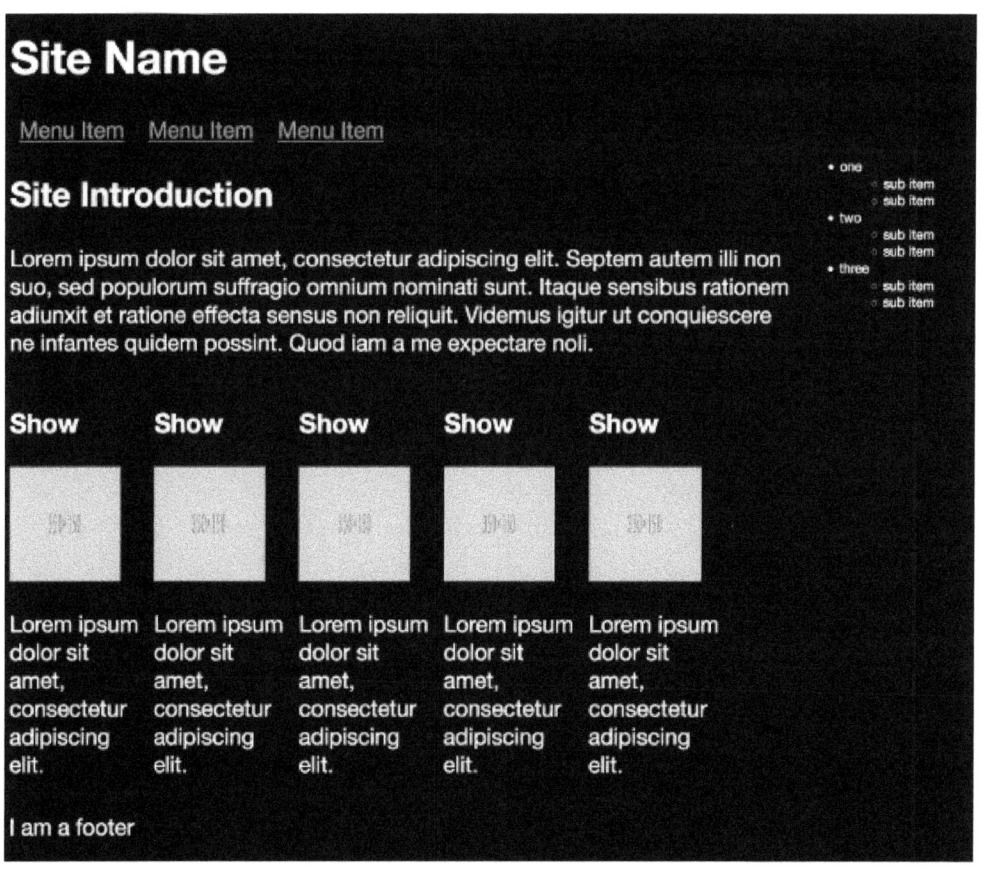

4-8. Rem cascade example

Other Relative Sizes

Sizes based on percentages, ems and rems are not the only options available to you. There are actually nine in total. Some are quite obscure, or not really necessary, but others are more useful after an initial learning curve. Take, for example, the vw and vh units, which are a percentage of the width and height of the viewport respectively.

There is also `vmin` (based on which is smallest of the viewport height and width) and `vmax` (based on which is largest of the viewport height and width). These are amazingly flexible, as the size will automatically react to the size of the viewport, but you can lose track of what sizes fonts actually are.

Take a viewport that's 1000px wide and 800px high:

- 1vw is 1% of the total width, i.e. 10px
- 100vw is 100% of the width, i.e. 1000px
- 50vw is 50% of the width, i.e. 500px
- 1vh is 1% of the height, i.e. 8px
- 1vmin is 1% of the smallest of the two sizes, i.e. 1% of 800px, which is 8px
- 1vmax is 1% of the largest of the two sizes, i.e. 1% of 1000px, which is 10px

Try adding the following to the body element:

```
body {
    font-size: 1.5vw;
}
```

Your base font size will now be 1.5% of your body width, which will depend on the width of your browser window.

At first, it looks like viewport sizing is the answer to your responsive dreams, but you'll notice that, as you shrink the browser window, the font size becomes unreadable, as 1.5% of a small viewport width is a tiny font size.

Of course, you could fix this with breakpoints, but then that defeats the purpose of using this sizing unit in the first place. There's a clever workaround for this, thanks to Zell Liew and Mike Riethmuller[1]:

```
body {
    font-size: calc(16px + 0.25vw);
}

/* The above won't work in Safari, but the below does */
body {
    font-size: calc(100% + 0.25vw)
}
```

This works by using the CSS3 `calc` function to calculate a base font size (16px or 100%) and then adding 0.25% of the viewport width to it, reducing the amount of variation between sizes as the viewport dimensions change. You're free to change both the values in the calculation to suit your needs.

> **Browser Support**
>
> Some viewport sizing and the calc functions are not fully supported in all browsers, with even recent versions of Internet Explorer and Edge not supporting the `vmax` property, and older versions of the Android browser not supporting all calculation types in `calc`.

For the remainder of this chapter, I'll use the em unit, but before refactoring the demo site text, let's return to typography and optimizing it for the web.

Creating Readable Text

You can use all the typographical properties outlined earlier in this chapter in conjunction with the sizing units also discussed, allowing for fine-grained tweaking of text to make it the most readable on any device.

---

[1]. http://zellwk.com/blog/viewport-based-typography/

There are, of course, many schools of thought on what "good text" looks like, and it depends on how much text your pages show and how important it is to those pages. The example site in this book has a small amount of text, so it's relatively easy to make it readable. Text-heavy sites such as a blog will need more thought and consideration.

You should consider what font faces, styles, sizes, and layouts suit various screen sizes and resolutions and balance this with any style guides your project may have.

Let's start overhauling the text of the demo site by tweaking the base text properties:

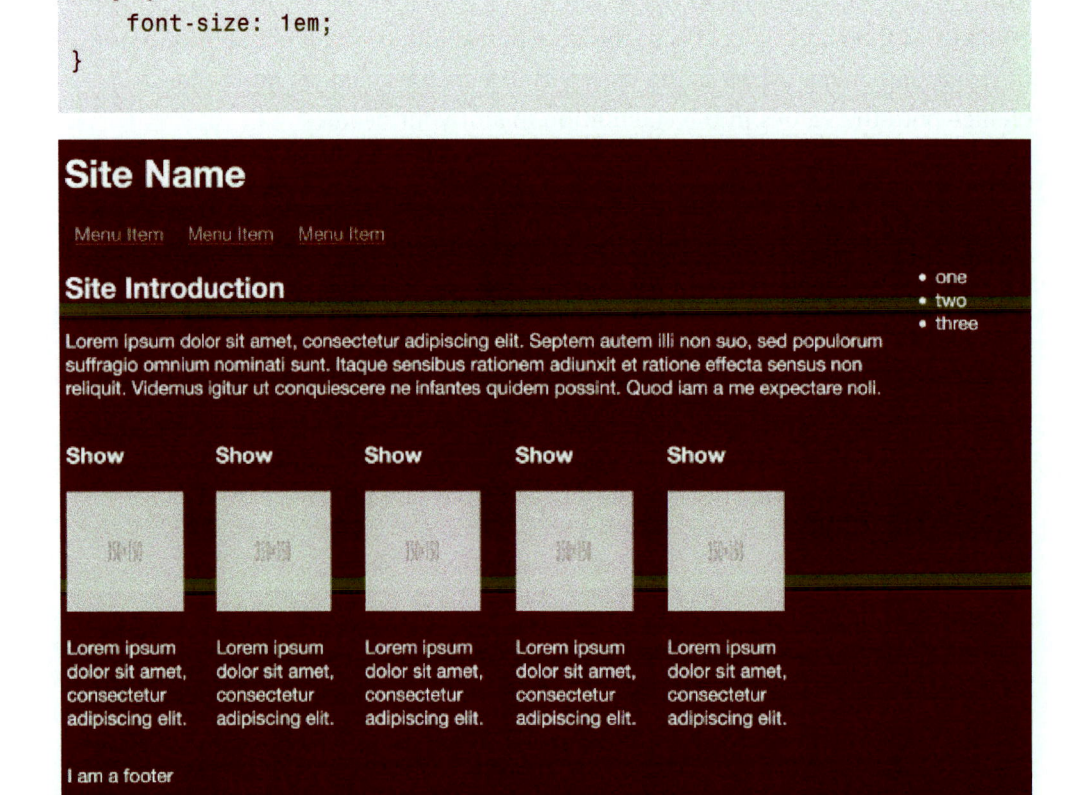

```
body {
    font-size: 1em;
}
```

4-9. Setting the font size

This sets the default font size to be the browser default, likely 16px as discussed earlier.

For the small-screen version of the page (that is, the default styles) the show description text is actually hidden, so we needn't worry about formatting it. However, the main site description is taking up way too much space when screen real estate is limited, so use a `:not` pseudo-class to reduce the default font size and exclude the show descriptions:

```
section.showslisting p:not(.showdescription) {
    font-size: 0.8em;
}
```

Site Introduction

Lorem ipsum dolor sit amet, consectetur adipiscing elit. Septem autem illi non suo, sed populorum suffragio omnium nominati sunt. Itaque sensibus rationem adiunxit et ratione effecta sensus non reliquit. Videmus igitur ut conquiescere ne infantes quidem possint. Quod iam a me expectare noli.

4-10. The site's intro text resized

As the screen size grows, apart from watching the videos, the show descriptions are likely what people want to access, so let's make the text slightly bigger to stand out more. With this medium screen size, still only a text summary is shown, so this is enough to make it more readable:

```
@media only screen and (min-width: 768px) {
    .showdescription {
        font-size: 1.2em;
    }
}
```

4-11. Show descriptions are now larger

As the screen gets larger, let's increase the text size and tighten the line spacing, especially as people may now be reading these descriptions from across the room as they settle in for an evening of entertainment.

```
/* Medium devices and desktops */
@media only screen and (min-width: 992px) {
    .showdescription {
        font-size: 1.3em;
        line-height: 1.1em;
    }
}
```

4-12. The full description text

Read On

In this chapter, I've introduced typographical concepts that are relevant to responsive design, and I've shown how they are represented in CSS. I've also covered the different sizing units that you can use to set these properties, and how to make important text on your pages readable. In the next chapter, I'll look at how to do the same with the rest of your page content, such as images and videos.

Chapter 5

Responsive Images and Video

The exchange of text-based content brought the web into existence, but images and other rich media have kept it evolving and made it what we all know/love/dislike.

Options for making images responsive has developed rapidly in recent years, with the ability to load images perfectly suited to users' devices. And the addition of new HTML elements like `video` has opened up new options for responsive design. It's fresh territory, but with pitfalls, compromises, and new techniques to learn. So let's get going!

Images

Images are a powerful communication device, portraying a message, intent, explanation, and bringing life to your web pages.

Images have also been a constant source of anguish for designers (web and print) for many years, and while HTML5 has brought a lot of improvements, adding responsive images to your web page still requires planning and preparation.

For this chapter, I've replaced the placeholder graphics used up to this point on the site with images from royalty free sites to represent what a site with real TV shows might look like.

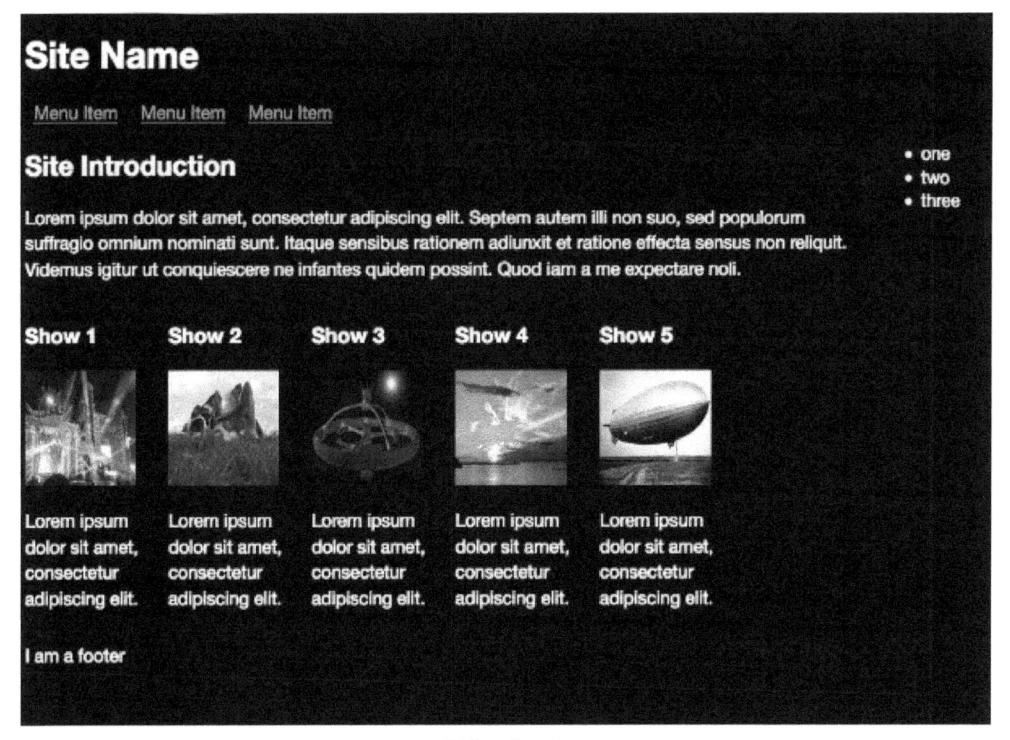

5-1. Adding show images

There are issues with the page now that we've added real images. The most obvious is that, while the layout is still fine, all the images are forced into the same dimensions, which means they aren't taking advantage of the available screen space. The example site is for browsing and watching videos, so it makes sense to make the visual content as prominent and easy to see as possible.

To show how to use responsive images, we'll change the demo site to have different image sizes and layouts suited to each use case at the breakpoints defined in Chapter 3.

First, change the CSS and HTML to better accommodate the images we'll be adding. Let's give the main content area more space and reduce the size of the aside menu:

```css
@media only screen and (min-width: 992px) {
    aside {
        width: 15%;
        display: block;
    }

    section.showslisting {
        width: 75%;
    }
}
```

Add the mobile first styles for the `divs` that contain details about a show. This sets a maximum width of 480px, centered, with an ideal width of *most* of the screen:

```css
section.tvshow {
    width: 90%;
    max-width: 480px;
    margin: 0 auto;
    display: block;
}
```

Next, add a media query for the same `div` when displayed on larger screens—still centered and filling most of the screen:

```
@media only screen and (min-width: 480px) {
    section.tvshow {
        max-width: 768px;
    }
}
```

As we jump to a larger screen, let's start showing more than one thumbnail in a row. This actually means that images will now be smaller, and the `max-width` of each `div` should be half the maximum screen size for this media query:

```
@media only screen and (min-width: 768px) {
    section.tvshow {
        width: 46%;
        margin-right: 15px;
        display: inline-block;
        max-width: 496px; /* The next break point divided by 2*/
    }
}
```

Next is the media query for larger screens, where we now show four items per row and adjust the `div` and image sizes accordingly:

```
@media only screen and (min-width: 992px) {
    section.tvshow {
        width: 22%;
        margin-right: 15px;
        display: inline-block;
    }
}
```

Finally, change the media query for TV and larger screens:

5-2. Chapter5/image_width/layout.css *(excerpt)*

```css
/* Large Devices, Wide Screens, TVs */
@media only screen and (min-width: 1800px) {
    section.tvshow {
    width: 46%;
    margin-right: 15px;
    display: inline-block;
    max-width: 900px;  /* The next break point divided by 2 */
    }
}
```

Okay, now that the containers for the images are sorted, we can focus on the images.

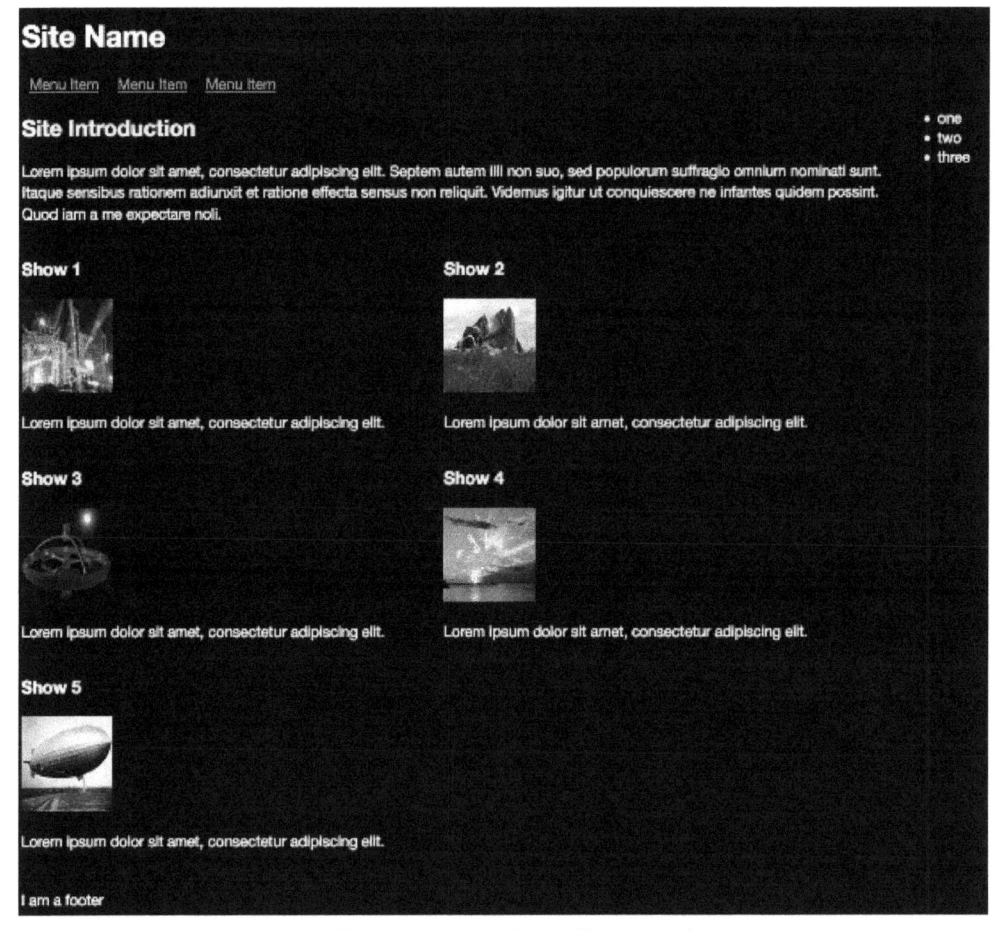

5-3. The page restructured at medium screen size

Responsive Dimensions

Change the image sizing to the following:

```
.thumbnail {
    width: 100%;
    height: auto;
}
```

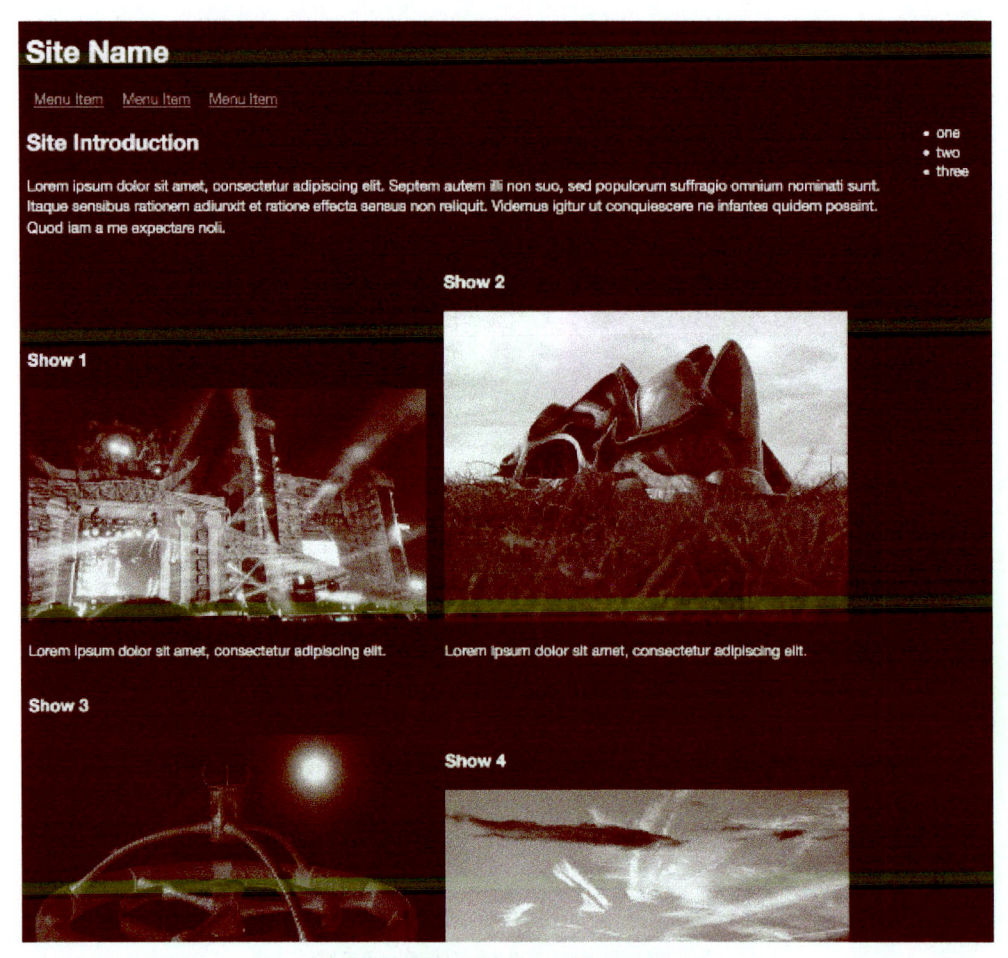

5-4. The effect of the changed image styles

This will set the image width to 100% of its container's width, and setting image's height to `auto` allows the image to occupy as much vertical space as needed to maintain its natural proportions. You'll notice that this means the images don't currently all have the same height, which affects the layout. You could swap these values to instead fill 100% of the height and fill the width automatically. Attempting to make images always fit precise dimensions can be a compromising challenge that depends a lot on the source of the images. If you're able, it might be best to edit them first so they all have the same dimensions.

Using `width: 100%` can mean that images will scale larger than their original size and render pixelated. To prevent this, try using `max-width` or `max-height` on the `thumbnail` styles relevant to each breakpoint.

So that's it, you're done, right? Unfortunately, no. Inspect one of the images in your web inspector and you'll notice that all we're doing is resizing a very large image. Even though it looks small, the actual file is still large, adding a lot of page weight. Look at the network requests: these five images total nearly **4MB**, which is a lot of data for a mobile user to load. To make your images fully responsive, you need to make sure the right file is served to the right device.

5-5. Image sizes

The Right Image for the Right Device

There are two methods for handling images responsively. One is `srcset`, an attribute to the `img` tag you know already, and the other is the new HTML5 `picture` element. Both methods use media query like syntax to select the image most suited to the device capabilities, but `srcset` allows the browser to make the final decision on what image to render, and `picture` explicitly tells the browser which image to render. For most use cases, `srcset` will be all you need, but for design heavy sites when you want more control over how a browser renders an image (e.g. cropping an image instead of resizing it) then using the `picture` tag will suit you better.

Much like the CSS rules loaded by your media queries, what image sizes you use and support is up to you and your use case. The example project is moderately well optimized, but could be better. For example, we could reduce the maximum size of images loaded on smaller screens. The queries can take the same format as those outlined in Chapter 2.

I created each of the images needed for the design manually, giving them a width roughly matching the maximum width the image will be displayed at:

- **Small Image:** 320px wide.

- **Medium Image**: 480px wide.
- **Large Image**: 768px wide.

Creating different versions of images manually is tedious, but gives you control over what gets shown in each image size. If you'd rather automate the generation of these images, there are several options, such as:

- batch processing in an image editor like Photoshop[1] or XnView[2] (Windows).
- batch processing with a build tool such as Gulp[3].
- using a plugin for your CMS or static site generator, which is likely a wrapper around the popular imagemagick[4] or OptiPNG[5] libraries.

srcset

Replace the existing image element with the following:

5-6. Chapter5/srcset/index.html *(excerpt)*

```
<section class="tvshow">
    <h3>Show 1</h3>
    <img src="../images/show1-medium.jpg"
        srcset="../images/show1-medium.jpg 480w,
        ../images/show1-small.jpg 320w,
        ../images/show1-large.jpg 768w"
        sizes="(max-width: 768px) 480px,
        (max-width: 1800px) 320px, 768px"
        class="thumbnail" />
    <p class="showdescription">Lorem ipsum dolor sit amet,
      consectetur adipiscing elit.</p>
</section>
```

---

[1] https://helpx.adobe.com/photoshop/using/processing-batch-files.html
[2] http://www.xnview.com/en/
[3] http://gulpjs.com
[4] http://imagemagick.org
[5] http://optipng.sourceforge.net/

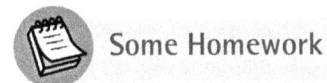

> **Some Homework**
>
> This example replaces one image, and to reduce repetition, I haven't included code for replacing the other four images. You can find the code for the remaining images in the code archive[6] if you want to try replacing the others too. Keep the media queries the same and replace the images with the appropriate files.

This requires breaking down, and the layout we're using also adds complexity.

The first part of the element is normal, as is the last `class` property, the second and third lines are the new syntax. `srcset` is designed to allow the browser to make the best decisions about what image to display based on information you provide it. Each pair in the second line defines the images available and tells the browser its width, appended with a w. The third line defines the viewport sizes you want to load a particular image at, and what image to load.

The example above declares:

- Up to a viewport width of 768px, load an image of 480px width.
- Between a viewport width of 768 and 1800px, load an image of 320px width.
- If no other rule applies, then load an image of 768px.

You can be more subtle with these declarations, for example:

```
<img src="../images/show1-medium.jpg"
    srcset="../images/show1-medium.jpg 480w,
    ../images/show1-small.jpg 320w,
    ../images/show1-large.jpg 768w"
    sizes="(max-width: 768px) 90vw,
    (max-width: 1800px) 24vw, 50vw"
    class="thumbnail" />
```

This instead declares that at the different viewport sizes pick an image that suits best a certain viewport width (vw) size. For this design, they are essentially the same, but it gives you an idea of how smart you can let your browser be. It's worth noting that this smartness can actually cause confusion when testing; I

[6.] https://github.com/spbooks/responsive2/blob/master/code/chapter5/srcset/index.html

have frequently found myself wondering why the tag wasn't working how I expected it to, only to realize that it was due to the browser holding on to cached version of the images, or optimizing for a retina screen, and again caching those images. To debug what's happening while figuring out your `srcsets`, I recommend using incognito / private windows, double-checking your screen resolution, and keeping developer tools open to see what files the browser is actually loading.

If this smartness is too unpredictable for you and you find yourself needing more control, then the `picture` tag is for you.

The `picture` Element

Try replacing the `img` tags with the below:

5-7. Chapter5/picture_tag/index.html *(excerpt)*

```
<picture>
    <source srcset="../images/show1-small.jpg"
    media="(max-width: 320px)" class="thumbnail">
    <source srcset="../images/show1-medium.jpg"
    media="((min-width: 320px) and (max-width: 480px))"
    class="thumbnail">
    <source srcset="../images/show1-large.jpg"
    media="(min-width: 480px)"
    class="thumbnail">
    <img src="../images/show1-medium.jpg"
    class="thumbnail">
</picture>
```

More Homework

As with the previous section, this example replaces one image, and to reduce repetition, I haven't included code for replacing the other four images. You can find the code for replacing the remaining images in the code archive[7] if you want to try replacing the others too. Keep the media queries the same and replace the images with the appropriate files.

We've replaced the default `img` with the HTML5 `picture` element. This element is still considered experimental (especially with Microsoft and older Android browsers) but should be widely used soon. Helpfully, the `img` inside the `picture` is a fallback image for browsers that don't support `picture`, meaning that the browser will load a default image if it doesn't support the newer element.

I chose the medium-sized image, as it's not too large or small, allowing for a reasonable level of responsiveness on unsupported browsers.

Supporting Older Browsers

If you want to add better support for older browsers, you can use a "polyfill" (a term for a library that plugs missing functionality). Specifically, in this case, that's Scott Jehl's picturefill[8].

One other useful application of the `picture` element, enabled through its inner `source` element, is to load different image formats, such as scaleable vector images (SVGs):

```
<picture>
    <source srcset="logo.svg" type="image/svg+xml">
    <img src="logo.png" alt="Logo">
</picture>
```

If the browser doesn't support SVG images, then it will load the PNG instead.

Another option is to load higher resolution images for high resolution screens:

```
<picture>
    <source srcset="../images/show1-2x.jpg"
    media="(min-resolution: 120dpi)" class="thumbnail">
    <img src="../images/show1-medium.jpg"
    class="thumbnail">
```

---

[7] https://github.com/spbooks/responsive2/blob/master/code/chapter5/picture_tag/index.html

[8] https://github.com/scottjehl/picturefill

```
</picture>
```

Responsive Video

Continuing the theme of semantic elements in HTML5, the respective elements for video and audio are `video` and `audio`. Since we're building a video site in this book, I won't focus too much on the `audio` element, but I think after using the `picture` and `video` elements, you'll understand how to use it.

The `video` Element

Many years ago, I made a site of music videos. This was prior to the widespread availability of broadband, and I spent a long time optimizing videos as much as possible to make them viewable on slow connections. I also had to decide what video plugin to use to display the video. Would it be best with Quicktime? RealPlayer? Or the tool that everyone loves to hate now (but which was popular at the time), Flash?

Those video format wars are largely over now, replaced by a series of standard formats and HTML5 elements, making a designer's life much easier, and also reducing that user-experience-killing process of having to download a plugin to view a video. The `video` element has a lot wider support than `picture`, with only IE8 and early Android versions likely to cause you problems.

However, the file formats supported by the video element still present problems, mostly thanks to vendors' differing attitudes to DRM and to which format is the "best" to use (each vendor preferring the format it supports or helped to develop). All browsers that support the `video` element support MPEG-4/H.264, which is a compressed format. But it's also proprietary, which means browser manufacturers must pay a license to use it. Support for the WebM and Ogg/Theora formats (which are open formats) is less common, with really only Chrome, Firefox, and Opera supporting them.

Here's an example of the video element in use:

```
<video width="320" height="240" autoplay>
    <source src="file.mp4" type="video/mp4">
    <source src="file.ogg" type="video/ogg">
    Your browser does not support the video tag.
</video>
```

It's a much simpler and consolidated HTML element than the options that existed before. It loads whichever video format is supported by the user's browser, or a default string of text if the the video element or the file formats it contains aren't supported. The `source` elements are processed in the order presented. So, in the example above, if the browser supports both formats, it will load the first one it sees. That's about it; there isn't much particularly responsive about the `video` element, except that it loads suitable video files with controls for them.

There are a few tricks you can try to make videos more responsive, but let's start simply by making the video player controls visible, adding a poster image (a thumbnail shows before the video plays), and removing the manual size.

```
<video controls poster="../images/show1-medium.jpg">
    <source src="../videos/show1.ogv" type="video/ogg">
    <source src="../videos/show1.mp4" type="video/mp4">
    Your browser does not support the video tag.
</video>
```

Early proposals for the `video` element included having its own media queries (like the `picture` element has, as we saw above). But the idea was dropped, meaning that different video files can't be swapped out for different devices. So the only real way to make the video responsive in any way is to use percentage widths, for example:

```
video {
    width: 100%;
    height: auto;
}
```

This will make the video scale to fit its containing element, and you could use a `max-width` property to limit the dimensional size it could grow to, or a smaller value, such as `50%`. However at larger screen sizes it won't prevent upscaling of the video, meaning it could look pixelated if sized too large.

Unless you specify otherwise, a video will start to download to your browser once the page is loaded (so that it's ready to view if a user chooses to watch it). Notice the potential network overhead with a video, which isn't great for mobile users:

5-8. The video file size shown in the web inspector

There's a partial solution to this problem: add `preload="none"` to the `video` tag:

```
<video controls poster="../images/show1-medium.jpg"
preload="none">
    ...
</video>
```

Now the video will only load when a user clicks the play button, allowing the user to choose when/if it's loaded.

In our code files, go ahead and comment out the `picture` element (for now) and replace it with the `video` element as shown above.

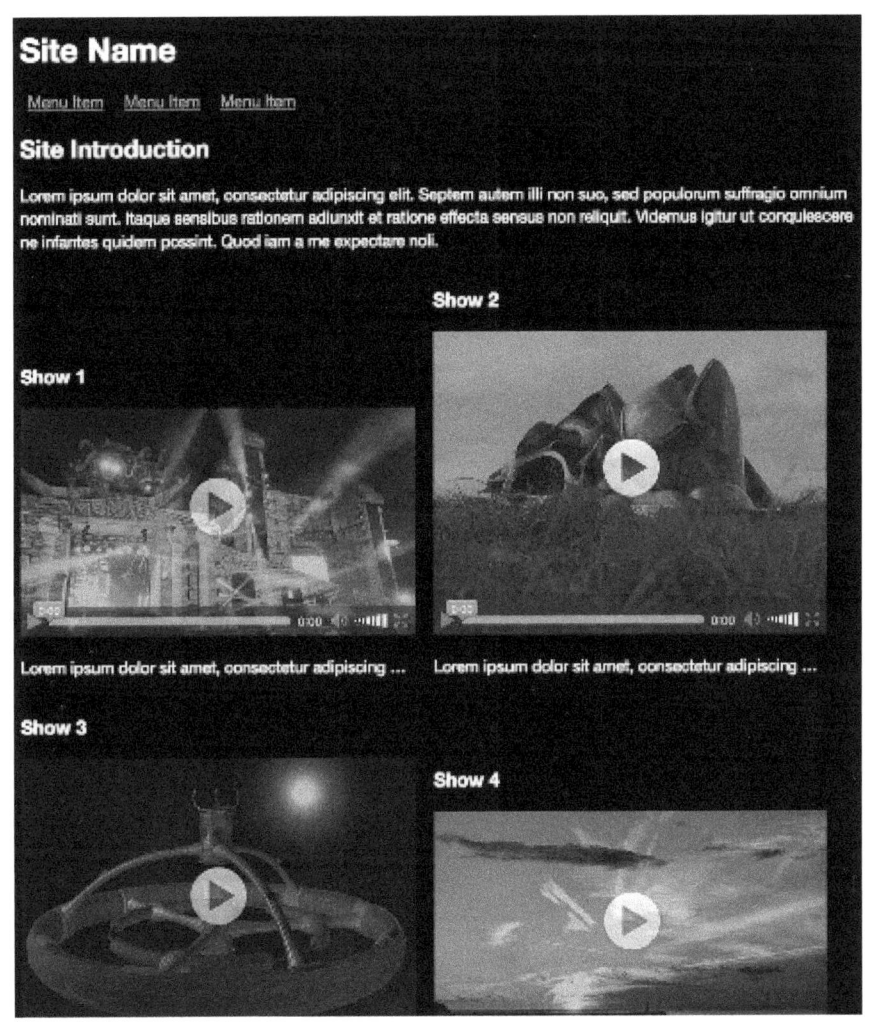

5-9. Videos loaded on a tablet device

If you use a larger video, then the video scales quite well at larger sizes. But you'll notice that at larger player sizes (the tablet and TV breakpoints) the poster image is pixelated.

There are no ideal solutions to this problem, and hopefully, better solutions will emerge as the element evolves. (One possible solution I'd like to see would be the option to set the `poster` image along with the `source` sub-elements inside the `video` tags, ideally with support for breakpoints and media format selective loading.)

Using a Larger Image as a Poster

Replacing the poster image with the large variant will mean the poster image scales across all file sizes, but it does mean that we're loading an unnecessarily large file at certain breakpoints.

If you want to style the poster element further (to change the dimensions or add padding), you can target it directly with the following selector:

```css
video[poster] {
    ...
}
```

Background Image

A way to create a responsive image representation of the video is to remove the poster image and then instead set a background image for the video, allowing you use media queries to load the appropriate image.

You'll need to set a background image inline within the `video` tag, or create a CSS style for each video to set the image, because *each* video needs a different image set as a background.

With an inline style:

```html
<video controls preload="none"
style="background: transparent
url('../images/show1-large.jpg')
0 0 / cover no-repeat;">
    ...
</video>
```

And with a CSS class:

```
<video controls preload="none" class="show1">
    ...
</video>
```

```
.show1 {
    background: transparent url("../images/show1-large.jpg")
    0 0 / cover no-repeat;
}
```

Using specific styles isn't a scalable option as you add more content, but for our example it's the best option. To avoid repeated typing on a production site, you'd probably use a templating system such as Twig[9] or Mustache[10], which would loop through the videos you want to display and populate the various file names as required.

If you don't want to use inline styles you could use a CSS pre-processor such as Less or Sass, which allows you to use functions and arguments (in this case, the background image) to generate the necessary CSS classes for you, but this will result in a lot of CSS classes.

To demonstrate the principle, let's take an approach somewhere between the two mentioned above, but without using any new dependencies. Add a class to each video, and then create the styles needed for the background image at each breakpoint. First, remove all the `poster` attributes from the `video` tags and add the class. For example:

```
<video controls preload="none" class="show1">
    ...
</video>
```

And the CSS for the mobile-first layout:

---

[9] http://twig.sensiolabs.org/
[10] https://mustache.github.io/

```css
.show1 {
    background: transparent url("../images/show1-medium.jpg")
    0 0 / cover no-repeat;
}
```

Then for larger mobile devices:

```css
@media only screen and (min-width: 480px) {
    .show1 {
    background: transparent url("../images/show1-large.jpg")
    0 0 / cover no-repeat;
    }
}
```

For larger tablets and desktop devices:

```css
@media only screen and (min-width: 992px) {
    .show1 {
        background: transparent url("../images/show1-small.jpg")
        0 0 / cover no-repeat;
    }
}
```

And finally for large screens and TVs:

```css
@media only screen and (min-width: 1800px) {
    .show1 {
        background: transparent url("../images/show1-large.jpg")
        0 0 / cover no-repeat;
    }
}
```

Now create matching classes and styles for each other video thumbnail. Phew! That's great for responsiveness, but a lot of code! You can find the complete example in the code archive[11].

Clickable Image

Another different solution to creating a fully responsive video is to replace the video player with a `picture` tag that, when clicked, loads the player. This allows you to use the best of all responsive worlds, but will need JavaScript. It will also allow you to add features such as opening the video in a layer above the web page.

First, add the `picture` and `video` tags together for each TV show:

```
<section class="tvshow">
    <h3>Show 1</h3>
    <picture>
    <source srcset="../images/show1-small.jpg"
    media="(max-width: 320px)" class="thumbnail">
    <source srcset="../images/show1-medium.jpg"
    media="((min-width: 320px) and (max-width: 480px))"
    class="thumbnail">
    <source srcset="../images/show1-large.jpg"
    media="(min-width: 480px)" class="thumbnail">
    <img src="../images/show1-medium.jpg"
    class="thumbnail">
    </picture>
    <video controls poster="../images/show1-medium.jpg"
    preload="none">
    <source src="../videos/show1.mp4" type="video/mp4">
    <source src="../videos/show1.ogv" type="video/ogg">
    Your browser doesn't support HTML5 video tag.
    </video>
    <p class="showdescription">Lorem ipsum dolor sit amet,
    consectetur adipiscing elit.</p>
```

[11.] https://github.com/spbooks/responsive2/blob/master/code/chapter5/video_tag/index.html

```
</section>
```

Do the same for each other show, replacing the images and video sources.

Now set the `video` element to be hidden by default:

```
video {
    display: none;
    width: 100%;
    height: auto;
}
```

> **A Note on JavaScript**
>
> The JavaScript code in this chapter and in Chapter 6 are mostly presented in isolation, as they offer separate options to experiment with. If you wanted to combine and use all of the examples together, you'd need to plan further, especially in trying to minimize the number of event handlers required.

Next, add the following JavaScript that adds a click event listener to the page. If a click is detected, the code will check if the click was on a thumbnail. If it was, then it calls a `toggle_visibility` function. This function shows the hidden video, plays it and then hides the image that was clicked.

Add the following JavaScript inside a `script` tag to the `index.html` file, which adds the event listener:

```
(function () {
    document.addEventListener('click', toggle_visibility,
    false);
```

Once inside the function, if the element clicked was one of the video thumbnails, then continue, ignoring all other elements:

```
function toggle_visibility(id) {
    clickedElement = id.target;
    if (clickedElement.classList.contains('thumbnail')) {
```

Next, you need to detect which image was clicked, find the relevant video for the thumbnail, start playing it and hide the thumbnail image.

```
  var v =
↪ clickedElement.parentNode.parentNode.querySelector('video');
    v.style.display = 'block';
    v.play();
    clickedElement.style.display = 'none';
    }
}
})();
```

And now, responsive images are replaced with a video player that by design stretches to fit. You could improve this by reversing the process when the video is paused.

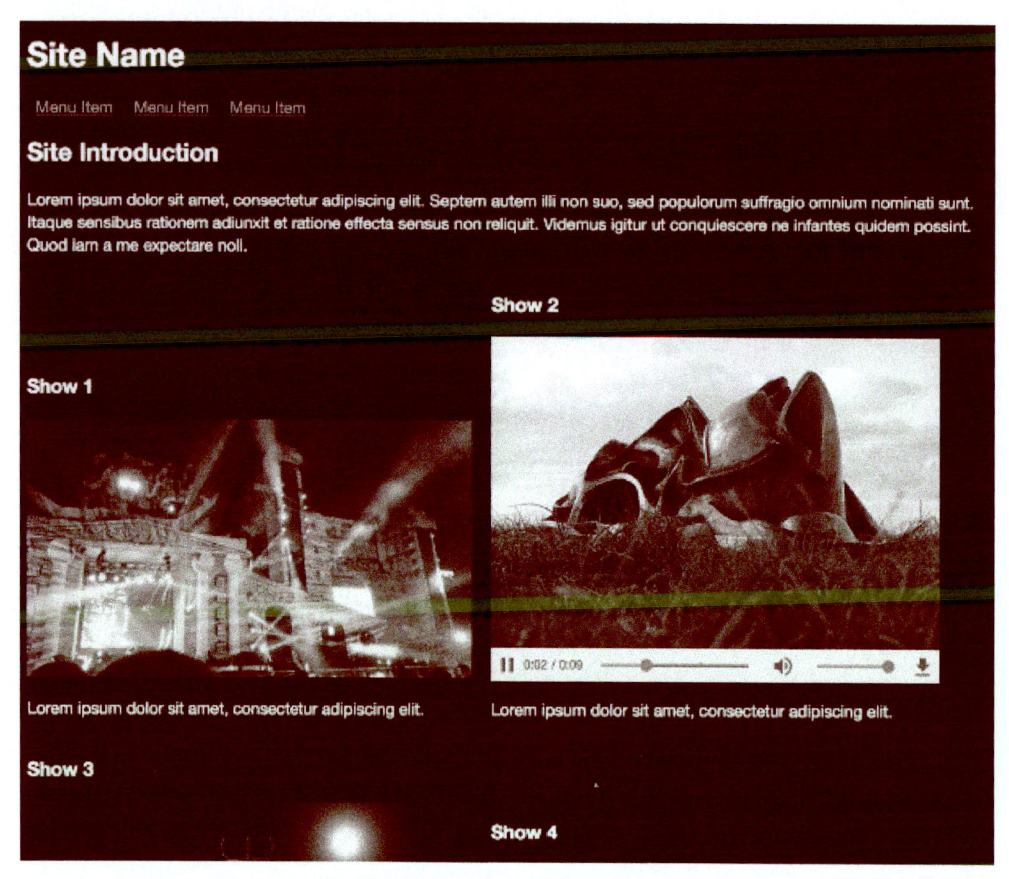

5-10. Clickable image and resulting video player

Get Visual

And there you have it: in this chapter, we've added a lot to flesh out the sample site with images and video, making it feel much more like a proper web page. As you can see, pictures are now a lot easier to make responsive. New tools and libraries have made responsive images much simpler and comprehensive than they used to be. Videos still require more work, but at least the days of complex media plugins are behind us.

In the next chapter, we'll polish the page with techniques for reacting to the capabilities of a user's browser, location, data and other "adaptive" techniques.

Chapter 6

Responding to User Context

Our example page is now responsive, and will work well on a wide variety of devices—scaling layout, images, media and text to suit.

In this final chapter, we'll look at techniques for adjusting user experience based on user context or preference. A real-world application would react to a lot of these situations from the back end, serving appropriate content to suit each case. Still, it's interesting to understand the different ways and reasons an interface can change, and I hope this chapter gives an idea of what's possible.

An API for Everything

Modern HTML and JavaScript let you check for a wide variety of parameters and then adapt what users see. The media-heavy nature of our demo site gives a lot of potential to vary how content is served to users. For example, family-friendly shows can be served up before a certain time of day, and more adult shows afterward; users can be offered the choice to play a video only if there's an appropriate internet connection available.

Based on Time

Some of the TV shows listed contain more adult content than others, and we should highlight them in the listings if it's earlier than 7.00 p.m. in the user's location, to indicate they shouldn't be watched by younger members of the family.

> **Modifying the HTML**
>
> I added the `evening` class to a couple of the `tvshow` sections. Go ahead and add the class to several of the `section` elements before adding the JavaScript below.

In `index.js`, add the following code to get the local time, and then extract the hour:

```
var localNow = new Date();
var localTime = localNow.getHours();
```

Now, build an array of all the elements with the `tvshow` class:

```
tvShows = document.getElementsByClassName('tvshow');
```

Loop through the array of TV shows and add the `highlight` class to any show if the time is earlier than 7.00 p.m. and it has the `evening` class:

6-1. Chapter6/time/index.js *(excerpt)*

```
var j;
for (j = 0; j < tvShows.length; j++) {
  if ((localTime <= 19) &&
➥ (tvShows[j].classList.contains('evening'))) {
    tvShows[j].classList.add('highlight')
    }
}
```

Next, write a CSS rule that adds a subtle highlight to shows you might want to exercise caution over:

```
section.tvshow.evening.highlight {
    background: rgba(255, 0, 0, 0.2);
}
```

Add a new `div` to `index.html` to let users know what the highlight means:

```
<section class="showslisting left">
    <h2>Welcome</h2>
    <p>RWDFlix brings you the best videos where and when
    you want them. <i>You are advised that shows
    highlighted contain more mature content.</i></p>
```

Another idea for responding to the time of day is to filter the level of blue light in the site to reduce eye strain or aid sleep, and the example later in this chapter that covers the Ambient Light Sensor API does something similar. You may have used applications like Flux[1] that perform this function on a system level. If you do offer this option, it should be something a user opts into and that doesn't happen automatically.

---

[1] https://justgetflux.com/

Battery Level

The HTML5 Battery Status API[2] allows you to check the current battery level of a device and respond accordingly.

> **Security Concerns**
>
> There have been recent security concerns surrounding the Battery Status API, so check the W3C specification[3] for news on its future.

Mobile devices (and laptops) are prone to running out of battery power just when you need it, so for this (mostly illustrative) example, let's help our users by noticing when their battery level is low and making the page less consumptive.

Darker colors *can* help reduce the battery impact on certain device screens (especially AMOLED screens), so the colors for the page are already reasonably battery friendly, but let's see how we can react to the battery level.

A JavaScript method is available to get a variety of information about a device's battery.

Add the following code inside the `index.js` file to check if the browser supports the feature. If it does, then get the battery level, which is a value between 0 (empty) and 1 (full):

```
navigator.getBattery().then(function (battery) {
    var level = battery.level;
    console.log(level);
});
```

If it's less than 20% (`0.2`), add a CSS class that reduces color brightness, and remove images from the DOM (since loading and displaying images can impact battery life, and every little bit helps):

---

[2] https://developer.mozilla.org/en-US/docs/Web/API/Battery_Status_API
[3] https://www.w3.org/TR/battery-status/#security-and-privacy-considerations

```
if (level < 0.2) {
    body = document.getElementsByName('body');
    body.classList.add('battery-save');
    images = document.getElementsByName('img');
    var i;
    for (i = 0; i < images.length; i++) {
        images[i].remove();
    }
}
```

Add the new `battery-save` styling to your CSS, reducing the brightness of the page text:

```
.battery-save {
    color: gray;
}
```

Whether color schemes actually save battery life is a controversial topic that depends a lot on the device screen, but it might be worth experimenting. Other, more definite ideas for helping users save battery are:

- reducing network calls and traffic
- reducing animations and effects
- reducing the amount of client-side processing by removing less essential JavaScript.

Although we removed images from the DOM with JavaScript, they're still loaded before being hidden. This contradicts the maxim of reducing network calls. As JavaScript only allows you to change an already existing page structure, you need to change what gets delivered to the browser in the first place. To make this work, you need to rethink the page structure to make it more mobile friendly.

Add classes to the current HTML to identify each TV show:

```
<section class="show1">
    ...
```

```
</section>

<section class="show2">
    ...
</section>
```

Now remove all the `picture` and `video` tags from each `tvshow` section, massively reducing the HTML file. Back in `index.js`, replace what is already there with the following code, which takes concepts we've already used in previous chapters (clicking the image for a video) and consolidates it:

6-2. Chapter6/battery_mobile_first/index.js

```javascript
window.addEventListener("load",function(event) {
    navigator.getBattery().then(function (battery) {
    // Get the battery level, and load images if enough
    var level = battery.level;
    if (level > 0.2) {
        // Find all 'tvshow' divs and loop through them all
        tvShows = document.getElementsByClassName('tvshow');
        var i;
        for (i = 0; i < tvShows.length; i++) {
        tvShow = tvShows[i];
        // Get the show name
        showName = tvShow.classList[1];
        // Create a picture element
        var newPictureNode = document.createElement("picture");
  // Set the source and classes for the picture, the code is
↪ identical to earlier examples, but the show name is passed to
↪ generate for each show
        var pictureInnerHTML = '<source srcset="../images/' +
        showName + '-small.jpg" media="(max-width: 320px)"
        class="thumbnail"><source srcset="../images/' +
        showName + '-medium.jpg" media="((min-width: 320px) and
        (max-width: 480px))" class="thumbnail"><source
        srcset="../images/' + showName + '-large.jpg"
        media="(min-width: 480px)" class="thumbnail"><img
        src="../images/' + showName + '-medium.jpg"
        class="thumbnail">';
        newPictureNode.innerHTML = pictureInnerHTML;
        // Add an event listener to the picture
        newPictureNode.addEventListener('click',
        toggle_visibility, false);

        // Also generate the video HTML in the same way
        var newVideoNode = document.createElement("video");
        var videoInnerHTML = '<source src="../videos/' + showName
        + '.mp4" type="video/mp4"><source src="../videos/' +
        showName + '.ogv" type="video/ogg">Your browser doesn\'t
        support HTML5 video tag.';
        newVideoNode.setAttribute("controls", "controls");
        newVideoNode.setAttribute("poster", '../images/' +
```

```
            showName + '-medium.jpg');
            newVideoNode.setAttribute("preload", "none");
            newVideoNode.innerHTML = videoInnerHTML;

            // Insert the new image and video in the correct place
    var nextNode =
↪ tvShow.getElementsByClassName('showdescription');
            tvShow.insertBefore(newVideoNode, nextNode[0]);
            tvShow.insertBefore(newPictureNode, newVideoNode);
            }
        }
    });
},false);

function toggle_visibility(id) {
    var e = this;
    var v = e.nextSibling;
    v.style.display = 'block';
    v.play();
    e.style.display = 'none';
}
```

When the page loads, it checks to see if the battery level is above 20%. If so, then image and video **nodes** (elements inside the DOM) are added inside each `tvshow` class, using the class name for the TV show to ensure the correct media files are loaded. If the battery is below 20%, only text is displayed. Ideally, you should add this functionality to a preference setting, so that users don't get an unwanted surprise.

This took some reorganizing, but now the page starts in a more mobile friendly state, only loading the heaviest page elements when the device is in a good state to do so. For the rest of the examples in this chapter, we'll use this concept to show how to add different detection capabilities. In fact, before continuing, try refactoring the time example to use the framework above.

Geolocation

The HTML5 Geolocation API[4] allows you to detect the rough latitude and longitude of a user's current location.

As well as providing great video content, RWDFlix also likes to recommend shows that may interest a user. This example will use the current location of the user to highlight shows that contain content about that location.

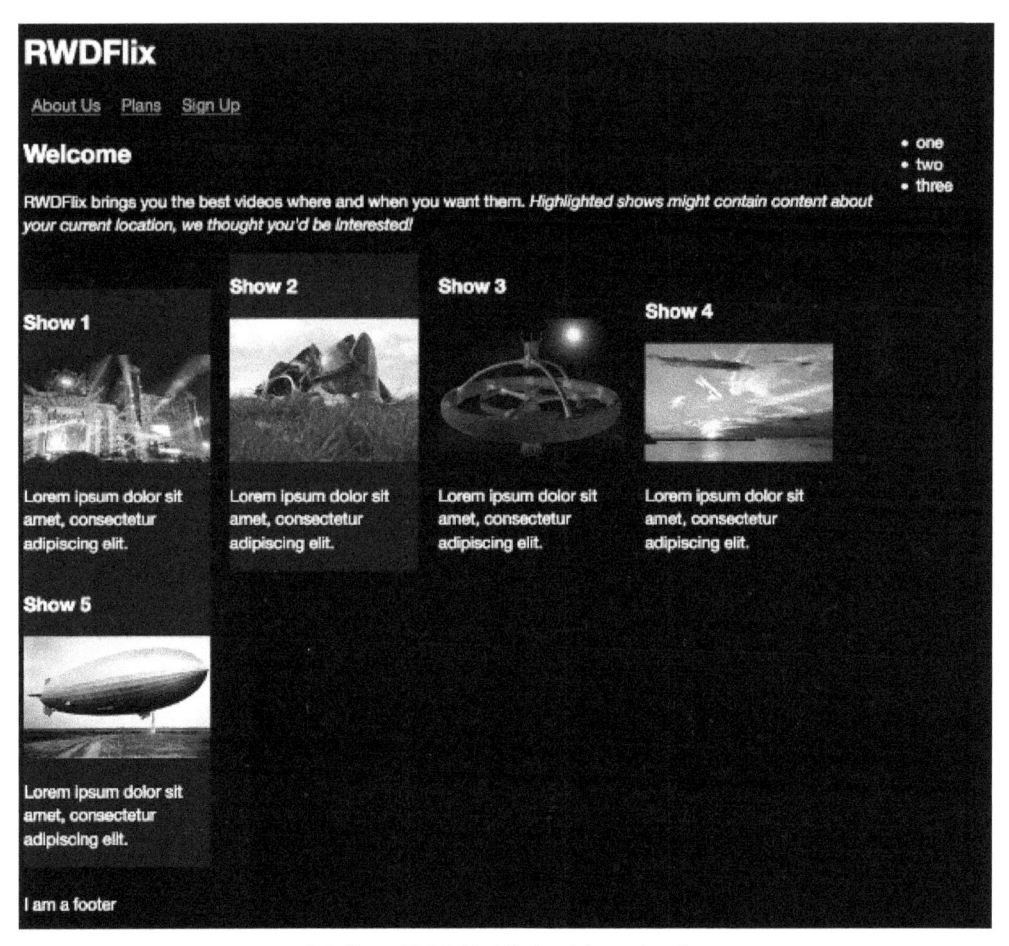

6-3. Shows highlighted that match user location

[4.] https://developer.mozilla.org/en-US/docs/Web/API/Geolocation/Using_geolocation

In `index.js`, replace the existing contents of the file with the following code that checks if the browser supports geolocation, informing the user if it doesn't:

```
window.addEventListener("load",function(event) {
    if ("geolocation" in navigator) {

    } else {
    alert("RWDFlix uses geolocation to recommend shows that may
    be relevant to you.")
    }
},false);
```

If the browser does support geolocation, get the current position of the user and pass the values to a new function:

```
if ("geolocation" in navigator) {
    navigator.geolocation.getCurrentPosition(getPosition);
} else {
    alert("RWDFlix uses geolocation to recommend shows that may
    be relevant to you.")
}
```

The API method returns the current latitude and longitude, which is not that useful to us, as we really want to know the current country of a user. Use the Google Maps APIhttps://developers.google.com/maps/ to turn it into a more useful country code:

```
function getPosition(position) {
    // Define the URL with the current latitude and longitude
    var url =
    "http://maps.googleapis.com/maps/api/geocode/json?latlng=" +
    position.coords.latitude + "," + position.coords.longitude +
    "&sensor=false";
    // Create a request and send the URL
    var xmlhttp = new XMLHttpRequest();
    xmlhttp.open("GET", url, true);
```

```
    xmlhttp.send();
    // When the request returns, process the response
    xmlhttp.addEventListener("readystatechange", processRequest,
    false);
}
```

Now that we have a result from Google Maps, we can process the results. We need to find the array that contains the country value, and then highlight TV shows that match that country in a similar way to the time example:

```
function processRequest() {
    // Is the response OK?
    if (this.readyState == 4 && this.status == 200) {
    // Parse the JSON response
    var myArr = JSON.parse(this.responseText);
    var i;
    for (i = 0; i < myArr.results.length; i++) {
 // Loop through the array of results and find the element we
 ↳ want, then continue when we find it
        if (myArr.results[i].types[0] == "country") {
        country = myArr.results[i].formatted_address;
        tvShows = document.getElementsByClassName('tvshow');
        var j;
 // Loop through TV Shows and highlight any that match this
 ↳ value
        for (j = 0; j < tvShows.length; j++) {
            tvShow = tvShows[j];
            if (tvShow.classList[1] == country ||
            tvShow.classList[2] ==  country) {
            tvShows[j].classList.add('highlight')
            }
        }
        }
    }
    }
}
```

> **Modifying the HTML**
>
> I added country classes to the `tvshow` sections. Go ahead and add some of your own before running this example. They need to begin with a capital letter.

Based on Network

The example site is a video site, and while we currently have the clickable images allowing a viewer to only load a video file when they wish too, we could make this more flexible based on the device's network connection. Or even better, we could create a preference that users can set if they want this feature.

The Network Information API[5] is not widely supported (currently only Chrome on Android), but browser manufacturers move quickly, so it may be better supported by the time you decide to implement it.

First, the easiest (and most supported) check is to see if the user is online at all:

```
if (navigator.onLine) {
    // Do something
}
```

Granted, this has limited use in the example, unless you want to check if the user has become disconnected before attempting to play a video. Still, it's a good idea to cover all bases.

While the Network Information API lets you check all sorts of values, it's not much use right now. There are third-party (paid) services for checking internet speeds, but currently, the "best" solution is using complex code to check how long an image takes to load, and calculate speed from that. I won't reproduce it here, but if you're interested, there's some helpful information on Stack Overflow[6].

---

[5]. https://developer.mozilla.org/en-US/docs/Web/API/Network_Information_API
[6]. http://stackoverflow.com/questions/5529718/how-to-detect-internet-speed-in-javascript

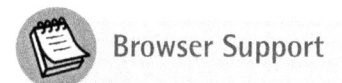

> **Browser Support**
>
> While the Network Information API is still in a draft state, it's an active proposal, so by the time of reading it may be better supported. You can find out its current status on the API's community group site[7].

User Preference

You have likely experienced **cookies** in your day-to-day web browsing. Cookies are typically used to retain state such as preferences. They can be set or read by the client or server and are transmitted within every HTTP request. This example will read user preferences and display page elements accordingly.

Often the browser will write a cookie when a user submits a form or undertakes some other action. For this example, we'll write a setting manually:

```
window.addEventListener("load",function(event) {
    document.cookie = "mature=no";
    ...
},false);
```

This determines if the user wants to see videos considered "mature" content. Using this value, we can use the same technique for selectively rendering TV shows.

To test, add the `mature` class to the end of the class list of a couple of the `tvshow` sections, and add `all-ages` to the end of all the others. In the `index.js` loop that renders the TV shows, read the cookie value and hide/show the appropriate shows:

```
for (i = 0; i < tvShows.length; i++) {
    tvShow = tvShows[i];
    var mature = getCookie('mature');
    if (mature == 'no' && tvShow.classList[2] !=
    'mature') {
```

---

[7]. http://wicg.github.io/netinfo/

```
    ...
    }
}
```

As all cookies are stored in the same property, you can use a regular expression to find and read the particular cookie you want:

```
function getCookie(name) {
    var regexp = new RegExp("(?:^" + name + "|;\s*"+ name +
    ")=(.*?)(?:;|$)", "g");
    var result = regexp.exec(document.cookie);
    return (result === null) ? null : result[1];
}
```

Ambient Light

Combining the Ambient Light Sensor API[8] with time detection could be a great way to adjust page or video brightness dependent on the time of day and the light available to a viewer. On many mobile devices, this is now handled by the operating system, but you could give it a boost or add similar functionality for computer users.

> **Security Concerns**
>
> There have been security issues recently highlighted with the Ambient Light Sensor API. I recommend you read the W3C specification to check its future.

Let's make an example that changes the colors of the page based on the current ambient luminosity (or the brightness of the surrounding area).

Replace the contents of the current `index.js` file with the following, which adds a class to the page body depending on the level of ambient light—the `luminosity` value:

---

[8] https://www.w3.org/TR/ambient-light/

```
window.addEventListener("devicelight", function (event) {
    var luminosity = event.value;

    if (luminosity <= 5) {
    document.body.className = "darkness";
    } else if (luminosity <= 50) {
    document.body.className = "dim";
    } else if (luminosity <= 1000) {
    document.body.className = "bright";
    }
});
```

Add these styles to your CSS file, for when a light is brightest:

```
.bright {
    background-color: #fff;
    color: #000;
}
```

This is how the page looks when this class is applied:

RWDFlix

About Us Plans Sign Up

Welcome

RWDFlix brings you the best videos where and when you want them.

- one
- two
- three

Agents of Shield

Lorem ipsum dolor sit amet, consectetur adipiscing elit.

Preacher

Lorem ipsum dolor sit amet, consectetur adipiscing elit.

Rick & Morty

Lorem ipsum dolor sit amet, consectetur adipiscing elit.

The Americans

Lorem ipsum dolor sit amet, consectetur adipiscing elit.

The Walking Dead

Lorem ipsum dolor sit amet, consectetur adipiscing elit.

I am a footer

6-4. Setting high contrast in bright light

This styling inverts the current color scheme to black on white to make it higher contrast and more readable in bright sunlight. If you have a modern device, you might have noticed a similar thing happening to the screen.

Next, add styles for the dimmest light level:

```
.dim {
    background-color: #6600b4;
    color: #b5aaff;
}
```

And here's how the page looks:

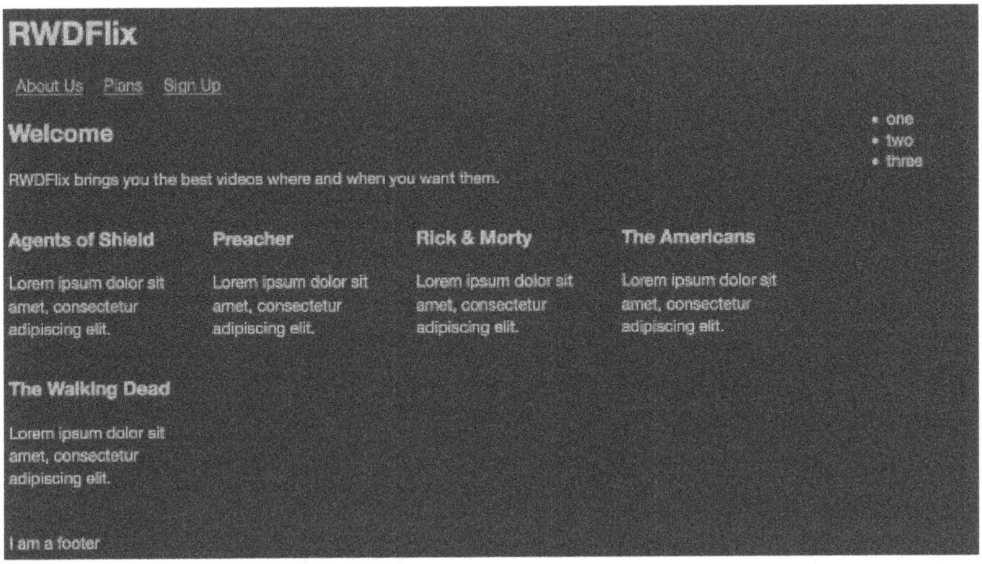

6-5. Setting low contrast in dim light

This makes the background and text easier to read in lower light situations.

Next, in a very dark situation, add a class that makes the contrast between text and background even less:

```
.darkness {
    background-color: #2d004f;
    color: #b5aaff;
}
```

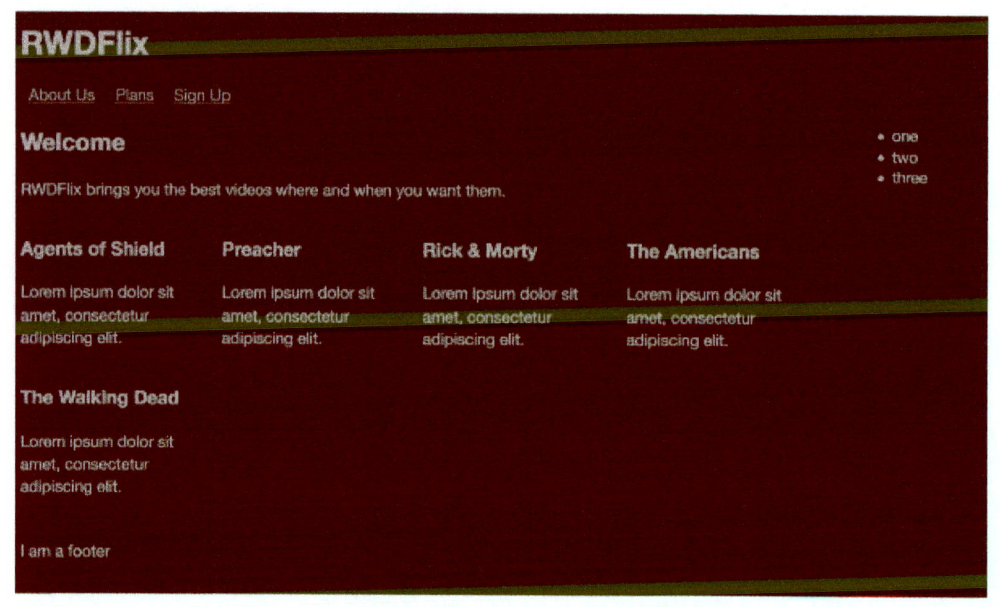

6-6. Setting low contrast for a dark setting

Rapid transitions between color schemes are disconcerting to users, so to make this less harsh, add the following CSS to the `body` element that eases the transitions between colors:

```
body {
    -webkit-transition: all 0.5s ease-in-out;
    -moz-transition: all 0.5s ease-in-out;
    -o-transition: all 0.5s ease-in-out;
    transition: all 0.5s ease-in-out;
}
```

Vibration

Another W3C innovation is the Vibration API[9], which provides access to a mobile device's vibration mechanism to provide tactile feedback. We could use this to add a more immersive experience to video playback by adding vibration to a soundtrack, but it would require a lot of work. There are other uses for this API

[9.] https://www.w3.org/TR/vibration/

that are handy for accessibility. For example, it can be useful if a device vibrates slightly when a button is tapped, letting the user know the action was detected.

Device Orientation

We've already seen how to detect and react to device orientation with media queries, but we could also react dynamically to device orientation. For example, we could switch a video file to a format more suitable for a landscape or portrait video.

If you want to get more experimental, what about controlling playback of a video based on the orientation of a device? For example, if a user tilts their phone in one direction, we could pause the video, and vice versa.

For this example, we'll create a new, simplified version of the page that's purely for playing one video.

Here's the HTML:

6-7. Chapter6/oreintation/index.html *(excerpt)*

```html
<!DOCTYPE html>
<html lang="en">
<head>
    <meta charset="UTF-8">
    <meta name="viewport" content="width=device-width,
    initial-scale=1.0, user-scalable=no">
    <title>RWDFLix</title>
    <link rel="stylesheet" type="text/css" media="all"
    href="layout.css">
</head>
<body>
    <header><h1>RWDFlix</h1></header>
    <main>
    <section class="showslisting">

        <section class="tvshow">
        <h3>Show 1</h3>
        <video controls poster="../images/show1-medium.jpg"
        preload="none" id="show1">
            <source src="../videos/show1.mp4" type="video/mp4">
            <source src="../videos/show1.ogv" type="video/ogg">
            Your browser doesn't support HTML5 video tag.
        </video>
        <p class="showdescription">Lorem ipsum dolor sit amet,
        consectetur adipiscing elit.</p>
        </section>

    </section>

    </main>
    <footer>
    I am a footer
    </footer>
</body>
</html>
```

And the CSS is equally simplified:

6-8. Chapter6/orientation/layout.css *(excerpt)*

```css
body {
    background: black;
    color: white;
    font-family: 'Helvetica Neue', Helvetica, Arial, sans-serif;
    font-size: 1em;
}

section.showslisting {
    width: 100%;
    margin-bottom: 25px;
}

section.showslisting p {
    line-height: 1.2em;
    word-spacing: 0.2em;
}

section.tvshow {
    width: 100%;
    margin: 0 auto;
    display: block;
}

video {
    width: 100%;
    height: auto;
}

.thumbnail {
    width: 100%;
    height: auto;
}

footer {
    clear: both;
}

/* Media Queries */
```

```css
/* Extra Small Devices and Phones */
@media only screen and (min-width: 480px) {
    section.tvshow {
        margin: 0 auto;
        display: block;
    }
}

/* Small Devices and Tablets */
@media only screen and (min-width: 768px) {

    section.tvshow {
        margin-right: 15px;
        display: inline-block;
    }

    section.showslisting p {
        line-height: 1.4em;
        word-spacing: 0em;
    }
}

/* Medium Devices and Desktops */
@media only screen and (min-width: 992px) {

    section.tvshow {
        margin-right: 15px;
        display: inline-block;
    }

    .showdescription {
        white-space: normal;
    }
}

/* Large Devices, Wide Screens, TVs */
@media only screen and (min-width: 1800px) {

    section.showslisting {
        width: 100%;
```

```
        margin-bottom: 25px;
    }

    section.tvshow {
        margin-right: 15px;
        display: inline-block;
    }
}
```

This results in the following layout for one video:

Figure 6-9. The video playback layout

Now add a `script` element below the page footer, containing the following code. This script initiates when the page loads, and accesses the video element, listening to whether it's playing:

```
<script>
(function () {
    var video = document.getElementById("show1");
    video.addEventListener("play", control_video, false);

})();
</script>
```

Add the `control_video` function, and assign the video clicked to a variable:

```
function control_video(e) {
    var v = e.target;
}
```

Check if the device supports the orientation API and if so, listen for changes to orientation. If it doesn't, then warn the user:

```
if (window.DeviceOrientationEvent) {
    window.addEventListener("deviceorientation", function (e) {

    }, false);
} else {
    alert("Sorry, your browser doesn't support Device
    Orientation");
}
```

Finally, react to the changes in orientation, pausing the video if a user rotates their phone to the right, and playing it again if they rotate to the left:

```
if ((e.gamma < -45) && (e.gamma > -90)) {
    v.play();
```

```
}

if ((e.gamma > 45) && (e.gamma < 90)) {
    v.pause();
}
```

📓 Getting Oriented

If you're interested in learning more about the three-rotation axis that exist in the Orientation API, I recommend reading "Using Device Orientation in HTML5" on SitePoint[10].

Responding to All

In this chapter, we've seen hypothetical examples of how we can change the contents of our pages to respond to the variety of sensors found in modern devices. These are always evolving, and I encourage you to keep up to date on the new APIs you can take advantage of in your designs to deliver tailored experiences to users.

This brings us to the end of our journey with this book. Responsive design is fundamentally about crafting pages that are usable by anyone, no matter what their device or circumstances. Whether it be screen size, performance or other factors, it's our responsibility to ensure that the user's experience is as good as it can be.

You're beginning your responsive adventure at a good time. There have never been better features available and soon to arrive in the HTML and CSS specifications—features for crafting experiences to suit the ever-changing landscape of modern web design. Some of these features are in flux, and their final forms undecided, but this also means you have the opportunity to test and shape their future. Get involved, and help create the Web you want to see[11].

---

[10] https://www.sitepoint.com/using-device-orientation-html5/
[11] https://www.w3.org/participate

Lightning Source UK Ltd.
Milton Keynes UK
UKHW051934260919
350509UK00006B/235/P